The Soviet Union

by W. GORDON EAST

Professor of Geography
University of London

A SEARCHLIGHT ORIGINAL

under the general editorship of

GEORGE W. HOFFMAN
University of Texas

G. ETZEL PEARCY
United States
Department of State

D. VAN NOSTRAND COMPANY, INC.

PRINCETON, NEW JERSEY

TORONTO   LONDON

NEW YORK

D. VAN NOSTRAND COMPANY, INC.
120 Alexander St., Princeton, New Jersey
(*Principal Office*)
24 West 40 Street, New York 18, New York

D. VAN NOSTRAND COMPANY, LTD.
358, Kensington High Street, London, W.14, England

D. VAN NOSTRAND COMPANY (Canada), LTD.
25 Hollinger Road, Toronto 16, Canada

Preface

Less than fifty years have elapsed since the Union of Soviet Socialist Republics, like the United States, made its revolutionary advent on the world stage, yet in its vigorous and articulate youth and more recently in its maturity, as a protagonist in world affairs, it compels close and widespread attention. The October Revolution of 1917, which yielded sovereign power, in the name of the common people of town and country, to revolutionaries who had hitherto worked underground or in exile, was greeted with alarm and dismay outside Russia. Certainly the cost of the revolutionary changes effected at first under Lenin and then under Stalin's long dictatorship were high in terms of human suffering, yet none can deny that drastic changes within the Russian Empire had long been overdue. A medley of nations, dominated by the Russians, was galvanized into a state, federal in structure yet markedly unitary too in political organization, by the Communist Party which had won the commanding heights of political power. The U.S.S.R., under Stalin's leadership, vindicated its viability, alike from internal strains and from the external assault of Hitler. Moreover, by applying a succession of Five-Year Plans, it released and harnessed the abilities and energies of the Soviet peoples and successfully carried out a policy of industrialization as it transformed Soviet society by providing equality of opportunity and of educational facilities.

This book outlines the nature of the vast Soviet land and the variety and distribution of its peoples. It shows how the Principality of Moscow grew into the Russian Empire—an empire which, like its forerunner, was endowed with remarkable powers to grow, both in population and in territory. How the Russian Empire collapsed during World War I and how the Soviet Union arose after its downfall—these too are described. Attention is then turned to the way in which, applying Western science and technology, the Soviet leaders set about to industrialize the economy, so that the U.S.S.R. has become an industrial giant,

with considerable promise of further growth and the intention to out-
strip the United States itself in the field of production. The contrasting
problem of inefficient collectivized agriculture, which continues to present
serious difficulties, is then discussed. Chapter 8 beats the bounds of the
U.S.S.R., notes how the U.S.S.R. expanded its territory as a result of
World War II, and indicates the vantage points and dangerous places
which lie along its extended periphery in two continents. Finally, there
is a brief discussion of the status in the world of the changed and
changing U.S.S.R. of Khrushchev and his successors: the place which it
already occupies and the yet higher status to which it aspires. In a world
where nuclear stalemate precludes all-out war, the U.S.S.R., the major
member of the by-no-means monolithic Communist bloc, is developing
and refining its economic diplomacy in the hope that it may win success—that is, political aggrandizement—by all means short of war.

Birkbeck College   W. GORDON EAST
The University of London

Contents

1   *The Soviet Population*

THE population of the Soviet Union early in 1965 reached about 230 million, a figure which was exceeded by those of only two other nations—the Chinese People's Republic and the Indian Union. Yet this high figure is much lower than it would have been but for the appalling population losses which the country sustained during the preceding half century. Before World War I the population of Russia had shown great powers of growth: it doubled between 1796 and 1850 and then doubled again between 1850 and 1910. World War I, which for Russia was followed by civil war, years of food shortages and even of famine, and the enforced collectivization of agriculture, caused immeasurable losses. The same holds true for World War II, when much of European U.S.S.R. fell under German military occupation. More than 30 million, perhaps more than 40 million, were lost during World War II alone, if account is taken of military and civilian deaths, emigration, and the deficit of births. The population increment to the U.S.S.R. of about 23 million by territorial annexations in east-central Europe as a result of that war was thus more than offset by these losses. The Soviet census of January 15, 1959, showed a total of only 208.8 million within an area which in 1939 must have contained nearly 200 million; but for World War II, the 1959 census total might well have exceeded 250 million. Another effect of World War II was to distort the sex ratio of the population, only 45 per cent of which were males in 1959 (although below the age of 32 years the numbers of males and females were equal).

The Soviet census of 1959 revealed that revolutionary demographic changes had taken place, mainly because of better living conditions and better medical services. The birth rate had fallen to 25 per thousand, which is about half the rate at the end of the nineteenth century. However, the fall in the death rate to 7.5 per thousand—the lowest in the world—reflects a fall to less than one-quarter of that around 1900. Since few people leave or immigrate into the Soviet Union, this means that its population is increasing yearly by 1.75 per cent, that is, by more than three and one-half million. Further, mainly as a result of the relatively high birth rate[1] and the very low death rate, the Soviet population contrasts with the aging population of western Europe in its high proportions of both children and men and women of working age. The working population increased during the 1950's by 1.9 per cent per year, although Soviet demographers expect this rate to fall slightly during the decades of 1960-1980. They forecast that the total population will increase at the rate of only 1.4 per cent yearly during the 1960's and only 1.1 per cent during the 1970's, to totals of 248 and 274 million in 1970 and 1980, respectively.[2] It is believed that the birth rate will decrease somewhat as living standards rise, as more and more people come to live in the towns, and as more and more women work outside the home.

Thus the U.S.S.R.'s position in manpower, whether for the armed forces or for the factories, mines, and fields, is specially strong— the more so when it is noted that women already share about equally in most forms of work. Life expectancy would appear to have virtually doubled since the Revolution of 1917. Great advances have indeed been made. Even if Soviet claims are not to be taken literally, they nevertheless mark a great achievement—one which has been made under housing and dietary conditions which still fall far short of the highest standards of the western world.

THE GEOGRAPHICAL DISTRIBUTION
OF THE POPULATION

Of course, the Soviet Union's vast area can clearly support large and increasing numbers, but most of its 223 million are actually

[1] The U.S.S.R. encourages large families by making grants to mothers for their third child and subsequent legitimate children.

[2] *United Nations Economic Survey of Europe in 1961* (Geneva, 1962), Chap. II, p. 50.

settled in only a small fraction of its territory. Like North America —with which the Soviet land compares in extent, range of climate, and natural resources—the U.S.S.R. includes a wide variety of environments of sharply contrasting values, actual or potential. At least one-tenth of the Union's territory in polar latitudes is too cold for more than scanty settlement. Yet Norilsk, a mining town with over 100,000 permanent inhabitants in 1959, has sprung up at latitude 69°N. In Central Siberia and Leningrad, town planners have conceived of an Arctic city to be built *beneath* a single foundation raised three feet above the permanently frozen subsoil. Forests, together with their contained marshlands, cover nearly one-half of the whole country. Here again, except in European areas long cleared for settlement and agriculture, these support very low densities of population, in mining and lumber camps and along the river valleys which allow penetration into them. Also, the considerable high mountain areas greatly restrict settlement, especially in the Caucasus, Central Asia, Eastern Siberia, and the Far East. Finally, and here comparison can be made with Mexico and the arid southwest of the United States, the U.S.S.R. includes considerable desert stretches in Middle Asia, as well as semiarid lands there and elsewhere.

Given the nature of this physical environment, with its hard, limiting, and, in places, forbidding conditions, it is not surprising that about four-fifths of the Soviet population is concentrated within about one-quarter of the Union's territory. This region might be broadly delimited as a triangle, with its apex at Novokuznetsk in Western Siberia and with two sides bounded by lines drawn therefrom to Leningrad and Baku. Eastward of this populous Russia, significant concentrations of population are exceptional and chiefly notable in the north of European U.S.S.R., in the oases and mountain valleys of Central Asia, and along the Trans-Siberian railway in Eastern Siberia and the Far East. Admittedly, there are also many minor pockets of population within the U.S.S.R.'s largely empty lands; also, the relatively early stage of development must be reckoned with. That small proportion of the Soviet lands which lies south and west of the Volga River, as well as the northern European U.S.S.R., have long been settled and exploited. Russian colonization in the Urals and Siberia, it is true, began several centuries ago. Even so, the settlement and economic development of the vast, scantily peopled Soviet territories beyond the Volga are processes very much of this century, and colonial effort of this kind, involving the redistribution of population as well as the application of capital, has still a long way to go. The pioneer, or rather the state-sponsored settler, is still much in evidence, seeking out new mineral strikes, peopling new and old towns, and winning new lands for the plow.

The geographical contrast, then, should be made between lands of old and relatively recent settlement. On the one hand, in the U.S.S.R.'s European, South (or Trans-) Caucasian, and Central Asian regions, villagers have long been working the soil and many towns have witnessed up to a thousand years of life. In contrast, in its colonial lands in and beyond the Ural mountains eastwards to the Pacific, Russians have carried out by stages (since about 1600 A.D.), conquests, colonization, and economic development to create a new world for themselves and for posterity. Behind this movement and giving it impulse was the land hunger of the Russian, Ukrainian, and White Russian peasantry. At low agrotechnical standards and with a high rate of natural increase, the peasants could not support their growing numbers and many moved east to settle and to farm. Since the 1880's, and especially after the construction of the Trans-Siberian railway, the scale and pace of immigration mainly of Russians, but also of Ukrainians, into Siberia and Kazakhstan increased. Many economic enterprises in Asiatic Russia were started under the tsars, but more striking have been the vigorously planned efforts of the Soviet government during recent decades. Not only have people moved eastward of their own free will and by inducements, but also as members of unfree labor gangs and as workers directly transferred. As a result, first Western Siberia, then Eastern Siberia, and later (and currently) Kazakhstan and the Soviet Far East have shown high rates of population growth. Even the U.S.S.R.'s North, which is variously defined but consists essentially of lands characterized by permafrost and by high development costs, has received its inflow of immigrants—namely, Russians who outnumber natives by four to one, in a total population estimated at between 3.5 and 5.0 million.[3]

These currents of population movement (made overland and also now by air), which may be compared with earlier seaward movements of Europeans to North America, have transformed visibly the Soviet map. The U.S.S.R.'s enormous Asiatic territories, notably Siberia and Kazakhstan, are no longer so empty and inert as they long were under the tsars. Rather, Siberia, including the Far East, has become an extension of European Russia, settled very largely by Russians and, to a smaller extent, by Ukrainians. Its population has increased more than fourfold in this century. In 1897, the first Russian census of Siberia, including the Far East, contained (in millions) 5.8; in 1926, 11.4; in 1939, 16.6; and in 1959, 23.6, of which Russians and Ukrainians made up nearly 95 per cent. Also the vast steppe and desert republic of Kazakhstan has drawn the Russian immigrant to its farms, factories, and mines; Russians, together with Ukrainians, accounted for a little above half of its population in 1959. In contrast, in the republics of South Caucasus and Central Asia, where many native civilizations have long been rooted, Russians have intruded in smaller yet substantial numbers. Table 1 shows these contrasts (see also Figure 1).

The steady growth of the Soviet population has been unequal geographically. During the intercensal period of 1939-1959, population numbers grew only slowly in the European territories and even declined in the Byelorussian and Lithuanian republics, but growth has been at a high rate in the South Caucasus and higher still in the Volga-Urals and in Siberia and Kazakhstan. The relative stability of population numbers in European U.S.S.R. clearly finds its explanation in the severe effects of German invasion and occupa-

[3] Terence Armstrong, "The Population of the North of the U.S.S.R.," *The Polar Record*, Vol. 11, No. 71, May 1962. On its widest delimitation the North occupies half of the U.S.S.R., with a population density of only 2.5 persons per square mile.

Table 1   *Russians and Ukrainians in Parts of the Asiatic U.S.S.R.**

	Total population	Russians		Russians and Ukrainians	
	(millions)	(millions)	(per cent of total population)	(millions)	(per cent of total population)
Kazakhstan	9.3	4.01	43.1	4.77	51.3
Central Asia	13.7	2.25	16.4	2.52	18.4
South Caucasus	9.5	1.01	10.6	1.06	11.1

* 1959 census.

tion during World War II and in the migratory movements and transfers of population which have continued during this century, stimulated greatly during and after that war. Estimates for January 15, 1961, show that over the preceding 22 years (i.e., since the 1939 census) the population of Kazakhstan increased by nearly 70 per cent, Central Asia's by nearly 30 per cent, and that of South Caucasus by 25 per cent. The increase for Siberia, too, was marked

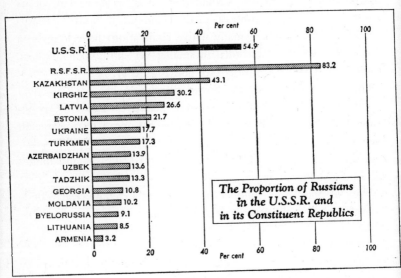

Figure 1

—about 35 per cent. For comparison, the U.S.S.R. as a whole added only 9 per cent to its total numbers in those years. In short, a large-scale redistribution of population has been taking place, which will continue to build up huge areas of dense population within formerly undeveloped and underdeveloped segments of Asiatic U.S.S.R.

Even so, these changes have not yet altered the historic fact that the European territory of the Soviet Union retains its dominance demographically and economically. Here, apart from the large tracts in the north, which remain by reason of climate uncongenial for agriculture and thus for close settlement, the densities of population are relatively high: in the Central Region, which includes Moscow and its ring of large satellite towns; in the Central Black-earth Region; in the Middle Volga; in the Ukraine and Moldavia; and in the Lower Don-North Caucasus Region. Indeed, because more than two-thirds of the population of the U.S.S.R. live west of the Volga, its western or European border is the most important to defend and the one to which the largest military forces can be most readily directed.

THE GROWTH OF TOWNS

The growth of population in the Soviet Union is now steady, but because it suffered catastrophic setbacks through war and internal disorders, it in no sense achieves the high rates of growth which characterized the United Kingdom and the United States during their phases of industrial revolution: hence, the paradox of labor shortage in the U.S.S.R. and its strong interest in automation. A remarkable and inevitable effect of Soviet industrialization has been the great growth of towns which contained 48 per cent of the population in 1959 and are expected to hold 55 per cent in 1970 and 68 per cent in 1980; earlier figures were 32 per cent in 1939 and 18 per cent in 1913. Even though the U.S.S.R. has still a very large rural population engaged in farming, its total fell by one-sixth between 1939 and 1959, and the outflow from the country lies behind the increase in both the number and size of its towns. In the 1959 census 4,616 of these were recorded, 299 of which had more than 50,000 inhabitants, 25 of which exceeded one-half million, four—Gorki (Upper Volga), Kharkov (Ukraine), Baku (Azerbaidzhan), and Tashkent (capital of the Uzbek S.S.R.) were approaching the million mark—and Moscow, Leningrad, and Kiev were the largest. Some of the more recently developed areas show the higher proportions of town dwellers—e.g., 54 per cent of Siberia's population live in towns, and the figure runs as high as 69 per cent in the Soviet Far East. The rapid rise of the urban population from 60 million in 1939 to 100 million 20 years later is explained mainly by three considerations: (1) the all-out Soviet policy of industrialization at all costs; (2) the mechanization of agriculture which has freed farm labor for the factories in the towns; and (3) the natural increase of population.

Some of the towns of today are the old towns of Russia, the Ukraine, South Caucasus, and Central Asia, regrown as the result of industrial expansion. Notable among these, with their 1959 populations given in millions, are Moscow (5.0), Kiev (1.1), Baku (with its suburbs 0.97), and Tashkent (0.91). Others are towns with at least a few centuries of life, such as Leningrad (2.9), and some of those along the Volga, in the central and southern Urals, and in Siberia. Many towns, in contrast, have grown out of workers' settlements in the application of economic plans during the Soviet period, and some of these are veritable boom towns: Magnitogorsk, with its iron workings and metallurgical plant in the southern Urals, which grew from nothing to 311,000 in 1959; Karaganda, on the major Kazakh coal field, which had 398,000 inhabitants in 1959; and Komsomolsk-on-Amur, the iron-and-steel center of the Soviet Far East, founded by the Young Communist League in 1932, which housed 177,000 in 1959. Figure 2 shows the distribution of the 148 towns whose populations exceeded 100,000 in 1959: the pattern picks out major settlement areas of the Union in contrast to the much larger expanses of tundra, forest, desert, and mountains where towns of this scale have scarcely yet arisen. The relative concentrations of large towns in European U.S.S.R.,

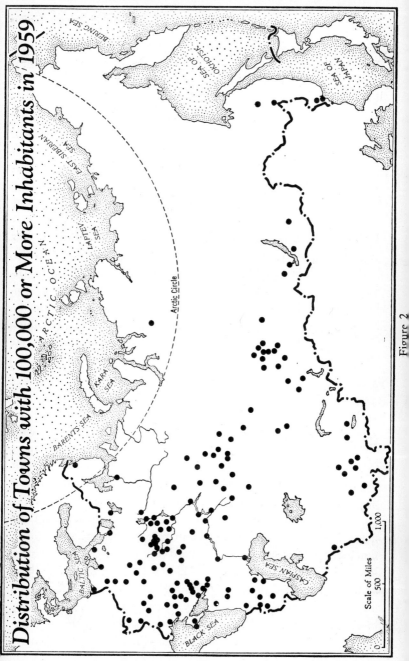

Distribution of Towns with 100,000 or More Inhabitants in 1959

Scale of Miles

0   500   1,000

Figure 2

15

Western Siberia, and the oases of Central Asia stand out on this map.

An unusual feature of the urban geography of the U.S.S.R. has been the continual changes of name resulting from either territorial accessions during World War II or, more especially, from the changing reputations of Soviet heroes. For instance, formerly Finnish Petsamo, on the Barents Sea, has become Pechenga, while Königsberg, formerly in German East Prussia, is now Kaliningrad. Examples of towns named after Soviet heroes who fell into disfavor are Molotov, which reverts to its old name Perm; Stalingrad (on the Volga) and Stalino (on the Lower Don coal field), which have become, respectively, Volgograd and Donetsk. (Donetsk was originally called Yuzovka, after the surname of John Hughes, the Welshman, who set up the first coke-fired smelter in Russia); Stalinabad, capital of the Tadzhik S.S.R., which is now renamed Dushanbe; Stalinsk in the Kuznetsk basin, which has become again Novokuznetsk; and Shcherbakov (on the Upper Volga) and Chkalov (on the Ural River), which are now again Rybinsk and Orenburg.

THE MEDLEY OF THE NATIONALITIES
AND LANGUAGES

In qualitative, as well as quantitative terms, the population of the Soviet Union raises points of special interest. It comprises many of the ethnic types which are commonly distinguished, but such descriptive classifications are of little interest geographically. It is much more important to note that its population is strikingly multinational: the 1959 census records separately no less than 108 nationalities, to which is added the item "other nationalities," which number, however, only 17,000 persons. But of the 108 nationalities, less than half (48 per cent) were 100,000 or more strong. With so many nationalities there are naturally varying levels of culture, numerous languages, and a medley of cultural traditions. Illiteracy has rapidly diminished during the last generation with the establishment of free universal education for children for seven years—

for eight years since 1960—and with provision for secondary, technical, and higher education. While the many languages remain in use, Russian becomes essentially the lingua franca throughout the Union. The Soviet Constitution of 1936 states that each nationality has the full right to use its own language and preserve its own culture, as it enjoys also equality of opportunity and equal citizenship. But since the Russians make up the largest group and were the creators of the Russian state, they clearly appear more equal than the others. It is significant that as many as 10.2 million people of non-Russian nationality recorded Russian as their native tongue in the 1959 census. Knowledge of Russian is clearly desirable since it increases an individual's chance of advancement.

The common use of the term "Russian" to denote a Soviet citizen, while understandable, can often be wrong. Lenin, it is true, was a Russian as is Khrushchev, but Stalin was Georgian, and Mikoyan is Armenian. Russians proper accounted for 114.6 million out of the total 208.8 million of the 1959 population—that is, 55 per cent—and clearly occupy the predominant position. They are widely distributed: most—97.8 million—live in the giant state within the federation, the Russian Soviet Federative Socialist Republic (R.S.F.S.R.). They form, however, substantial minorities in the other republics (see Table 1 and Map 1)—for example, 26.6 per cent in Latvia, 21.7 per cent in Estonia, and 17.7 per cent in the Ukraine. They have the smallest percentage in Lithuania (8.5 per cent) and in Armenia (3.2 per cent). Although the Russians are everywhere and have taken the lead during the Soviet period of revolutionary social and economic change, it should be remembered that the main spearhead throughout the Union is always the Communist Party, whose members, numbering 8.7 million in 1961, are recruited regardless of nationality.

Apart from the Russians, the two next largest groups are the Ukrainians and the Byelorussians, or White Russians (see Figure 3). Ukrainians numbered 37 million in 1959, of whom 32 million lived in the Ukraine S.S.R., leaving 5 million in the other states of the Union, mainly in the R.S.F.S.R. Byelorussians totaled 7.8 mil-

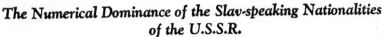

The Numerical Dominance of the Slav-speaking Nationalities of the U.S.S.R.

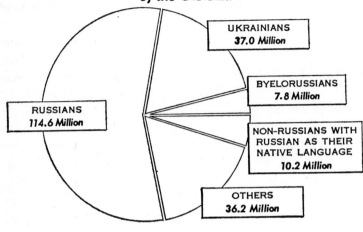

UKRAINIANS
37.0 Million

BYELORUSSIANS
7.8 Million

RUSSIANS
114.6 Million

NON-RUSSIANS WITH
RUSSIAN AS THEIR
NATIVE LANGUAGE
10.2 Million

OTHERS
36.2 Million

Figure 3

lion, and of these only 1.4 million lived outside their own republic.
Russians, Ukrainians, and Byelorussians have something in common in that they each speak a Slav language and that they make up today a higher proportion than formerly of the total population. Together they make up 76 per cent; the corresponding figure was only 66 per cent in the Russia of 1897.

There are 16 other nationalities whose numbers exceed one million: the largest, with their numbers given in millions, are: Uzbeks (6.0), Tartars (5.0), Georgians (3.6), Kazakhs (3.6), Azerbaidzhanians (2.9), Armenians (2.8), Lithuanians (2.3), Jews (2.3), and Moldavians (who are Rumanians so disguised—2.2). For the rest, there is a range of European peoples—Germans, Poles, Bulgarians, Finns, Greeks—and even (in the thousands) Albanians, Yugoslavs, Spaniards, and Italians. Asiatics are represented by Chinese, Koreans, Mongols, Afghans, Iranians, Kurds, and Japanese. In addition, numbering hundreds or tens of thousands, are many peoples who have preserved their national identity in the North and South Caucasus regions; others similarly in the Volga-Ural region of the European U.S.S.R.; and yet others, formerly among the most primitive, the reindeer herders and fishermen of the far north.

Language provides the clearest differential between the Soviet peoples. Languages of the Indo-European family claim about four-fifths of the population. The Slavic subgroup, we have seen, is dominant, but there are four other subgroups: the Baltic, Iranian, Armenian, and Romance. The Latvians and the Lithuanians, each of whom forms a separate republic, speak Baltic languages. Iranian (Persian) is represented by the Tadzhiks and Ossetians, who also have recognition in the political organization of the Union. Armenians form another subgroup, and they make up a constituent republic. Lastly, within the Indo-European family are some who speak Romance languages, namely Moldavians and a few French and Italians.

At least eight nationalities speak languages within the Turkic family, and they account for 8 per cent of total numbers. The chief subgroups are the Tatars, five million strong, who are established mainly in the Middle (or forest) Volga region; and the Bashkirs, formerly nomadic herdsmen, who are now settled in the steppe country south of the Ural Mountains. In addition, Turkic languages are spoken by the Azerbaidzhanians (in the South Caucasus), the Uzbeks, Kazakhs, Kirghiz, and Turkmen of Middle Asia, and by the Yakuts, now only 237,000 in number, in Eastern Siberia.

People speaking languages of the Finnic family make up between five and six million and include the Komi, the Mordvinians, the Chuvash, the Estonians, the Karelians, the Lapps, and the Nentsy of the far north, who were formerly called Samoyeds. The only other family represented by a few million people is the Caucasian, of which the Georgians are the principal subgroup. However, at least five other subgroups exist in the North Caucasus region. Finally, the Mongolian language family includes the Kalmyks, living west of the Lower Volga, and the Buryats, who live in south-central Siberia, to the east of Lake Baikal.

ATHEISM VERSUS RELIGION

Religion, like language, persists as a cultural differential within the Soviet Union, despite the atheistic position assumed by Soviet communism. The state church of the Russian Empire—the Russian Orthodox Church—was disestablished in 1918. While the Soviet Union has always regarded institutional and personal religion as an obstacle to its totalitarian aim, its policy has followed a deviating course dictated by expediency. On the one hand, it has persecuted and liquidated priests; confiscated Church property; secularized churches, synagogues, and temples; and launched vigorous antireligious propaganda, notably that of the League of the Militant Godless in the 1930's. On the other hand, the regime found that it needed the support of the Russian Orthodox Church, notably during and after the years of the Nazi peril. Accordingly, Stalin restored to this Church the office of Patriarch, and by this means and by other concessions, insured the support of the Church as a cobelligerent in the "Great Patriotic War" against Hitler. Also, the services of the Church leaders were needed in those western territories, populated by large numbers of Orthodox Christians, which the Red Army occupied and the U.S.S.R. retained after the war. With this aid, for example, the U.S.S.R. was able to bring to an end the ecclesiastical independence of the Ukrainian Orthodox Church with its potentially separatist tendencies. Further, in order to impress the western world and to assist his foreign policy, Stalin entered into a concordat with the Russian Orthodox Church in 1943, which allowed it to elect its Patriarch, restore its Holy Synod, publish a journal, open a restricted number of seminaries, and even own property. Similarly, the former vigorous assaults on other religious groups, notably the Moslems, the Armenian Christian Church, and the Buddhists, have been abandoned because it was realized that the leaders of such bodies can become valuable agents of Soviet foreign policy. The League of the Militant

Godless was disbanded in 1941, when the regime needed to rally support from every quarter, but an All-Union Society for the Dissemination of Scientific and Political Knowledge was set up in 1947 to promote atheism by more subtle methods.

Although the Soviet government has had some success in harnessing religious institutions to its wheel and doubtless has successfully indoctrinated most of its younger citizens, it has failed wholly to replace the belief in God by its own atheistic, amoral, and materialistic creed. Without doubt the number of believers in the U.S.S.R. has sharply declined since the Revolution of 1917 —as indeed they have done elsewhere. But the number of those who cherish spiritual values, even though they form a depressed class, remains substantial. Apart from the largest group—the Russian Orthodox Christians and their sect, the Old Believers—there are Roman Catholics; Protestants, notably Lutherans, as found in Latvia and Estonia; plus those Christians with their own independent churches in Georgia and Armenia. In addition, many millions of Turkic-speaking peoples are traditionally Moslems: these include the Azerbaidzhanians, Dagestani, Tatars, Bashkirs, Kazakhs, Uzbeks, Kirghiz, and Turkmen. The first named were— and some remain—Shiite Moslems; the rest are Sunnites. There are also Jews,[4] whose recorded numbers declined sharply as a result of German wartime occupation of west European U.S.S.R.; some Lamaist Buddhists among the Buryats, Tuvinians, and Kalmyks; and even some Shamanists.

SOME SOVIET POPULATION PROBLEMS

In conclusion, several problems arise for comment from this short review of the Soviet population. How adequate is the Soviet population to the needs of the state, which seeks to redistribute it geographically in order to maximize industrial effort, expand agricultural production, and to exploit hitherto untapped, or little tapped, resources? Does the existence of so many cultural groups of unequal size weaken the unity and strength of the Union? Do

[4] Moscow may in fact still be the second Jewish city after New York.

the many religious faiths, which evade suppression, seriously challenge the totalitarian regime? Do some peoples still occupy, as they did under the tsars, a colonial status? Are there nations within the Soviet Union who still aspire to independent national statehood? Or has a Soviet patriotism emerged which overrides narrowly national sentiments?

Only brief answers to these questions can be given here. It may first be noted that the youthfulness and relatively high rate of growth of the Soviet population insure increasing supplies of man-power and that much has been done, and continues to be done, to fit Soviet workers to the needs of the economy and the armed forces. Obviously, the Russians are the dominant group within the state and have taken the greatest share in educating, guiding, and stimulating the various other peoples—many of whom were back-ward or even primitive—towards modern industrialized life. Al-though this is a task which might merit the term "colonial," it should be recalled that the Communist Party cuts across national divisions and is open to a selection of all comers. Subject to the vigilant and powerful control exercised from Moscow, national autonomy within strict limits is conceded to the major national groups. Certainly, some of these at different times have had to carry out changes designed to fulfill all-Union objectives, which were resented and vainly resisted (for example, when certain Central Asian republics were required to grow cotton rather than wheat). Yet during the onslaught of Hitler's armies in World War II, only relatively minor national incidents challenged the solidarity of the regime in its efforts to ward off this external at-tack: several sizable groups—the Crimean Tatars, the Volga Ger-mans, the Kalmyks, and the Chechen-Ingush—were transferred to rear areas, allegedly either for their failure to co-operate or for the better security of the state. And although Stalin used all means to fortify his defense effort—for example, by recalling the achieve-ments of former Russian generals and heroes (some were even saints of the Orthodox Church) and by co-operating with the leaders of the Church—his regime was sufficiently established to withstand this supreme test: enemy occupation of many of the most productive lands.

Nor does it appear, now that all citizens except the elderly have known only Soviet rule and must recognize undoubted material progress, that national aspirations to independent statehood have any strong local foundation, whatever delusions may be nourished by emigré groups elsewhere.[5] In short, an overriding Soviet loyalty has developed, and much has been accomplished in ridding nationalisms of their narrower and exclusive bases. Certainly the contrast is sharp between Europe west of the U.S.S.R., with its many independent states, slowly feeling their way towards multinational co-operation within larger territorial frames, and the U.S.S.R., which claims to have solved its nationalities problem. Granted, this has been done by means often forceful and at times ruthless, which the western world is disinclined to adopt. In particular, the Soviet attitude to religion, which springs from hatred and fear and is expressed in a policy of cynical opportunism, inevitably restricts the freedom of national groups which the Soviet Constitution proudly proclaims.

2   *The Land of the Soviets*

THE Soviet population, though numerous, makes up only a modest fraction of mankind—7 per cent—but the land which it inhabits bulks much larger, amounting to 17 per cent of the inhabited surface of the earth. The Soviet peoples occupy a vast subcontinental territory of 8.6 million squares miles, which necessarily comprises a wide variety of contrasting yet complementary environments. These find distinctiveness through climate,

[5] Exception may be made of Estonia, Latvia, and Lithuania, but emigration and deportation of their nationals must have weakened their national hopes.

vegetation cover, altitude, land forms, soils, and, not least, geographical position.

The whole territory is distended east to west for more than one-third of the way around the globe. It stretches through 158 degrees of longitude from the Bering Strait, its most easterly point to its most westerly, where the boundaries of the Ukraine S.S.R. project towards Budapest in east-central Europe. To the north it borders inner seas of the North Atlantic and Arctic oceans: in the extreme north—at that mathematical point known as the North Pole—these waters meet those which extend northward from Canada. Southward it reaches the shores of the Black and Caspian seas and beyond the Caucasus ranges, while it penetrates the lofty mountain system of Central Asia. Certainly the U.S.S.R. controls abundant space; this space, however, has sharply different values for human habitation from place to place. Also its parts differ widely in their stages of development: the contrast is great between the smaller part, in Europe west of the Volga, which has long been settled by peasants and townsmen, and the greater part, mainly in Asia, which only now is undergoing rapid transformation.

The location of the U.S.S.R.'s territory deserves further consideration. In latitude it stretches at most through 42° from its most southerly boundary in Central Asia (at 36°N) to its central Siberian shores beyond the Arctic Circle. This is equivalent to the latitudinal range from Las Vegas to the northernmost parts of Canada and Greenland. The Arctic Ocean long appeared as a complete natural obstacle between North America and the Russian Empire. Air navigation and the opening up of the northern sea route through the Soviet Arctic seas in summer have, however, revealed the proximity of the U.S.S.R. to northern North America. It is now necessary to draw maps on suitable projections showing this relationship, in addition to that more familiar relationship with Europe and Asia, within both of which it lies. Figure 4 shows the Soviet land as it is fittingly presented in its world setting to Soviet school children. That the U.S.S.R. bestrides two continents as these are conventionally defined is not a matter of

Figure 4

practical importance. It merely recognizes that, for valid reasons of cultural geography, Europe and Asia have long been recognized as distinct, although Europe is clearly only a peninsular projection of what is one continuous land mass (*Erdteil*) which is conveniently called Eurasia. Was not Dostoevski right in insisting that Russia was neither part of Europe nor part of Asia, but a world apart?

The U.S.S.R. has about 30,000 miles of coasts and extends its territory and jurisdiction 12 nautical miles seawards into what are called its territorial seas. The many seas which it abuts have unequal value for reasons of climate and proximity to populous areas. At best, the inner seas of the Arctic Ocean offer water access to and from northern Siberia for three months in summer. (The warming up that has taken place in this century in these latitudes must have helped the U.S.S.R.'s use of these seas.) The White Sea freezes for several months; farther west, however, the Barents Sea, which gives direct access to the North Atlantic, receives some winter amelioration from the North Atlantic drift, so that Murmansk, naval base and fishing port, is open all year. This sea is also valuable for its fisheries. Southward from the Bering Strait, the U.S.S.R. has a long Pacific coast, which virtually encloses the Sea of Okhotsk and fronts also the Sea of Japan. These two seas support large fishing industries, but most of the coast is mountainous and blocked by ice for most of the year and hampered by fog in summer. Only in the extreme south does Vladivostok manage to keep open throughout the year with the aid of icebreakers. The Soviet Baltic coasts, which give access to the Atlantic via the Danish Straits, suffer also from the winter freeze. In contrast, the Azov and Black seas suffer little from freezing and open a way to the Danube River, to the Mediterranean basin, and thus also to the Suez Canal. The landlocked Caspian, useful for interregional shipments, is slowly shallowing, since evaporation exceeds the inflow from rivers, increasingly as the waters of the Volga are stored for use in irrigation. The Azov, Black, and Caspian seas all substantially add to the Soviet fish catch, and off the Caspian coast near Baku oil is piped from beneath the sea bed.

Climate, wrote Montesquieu, is the first of all the empires. Certainly in the U.S.S.R., which includes large areas of permafrost and parched desert and suffers widely from the winter freeze of rivers and seaports, climate imposes rigorous limits on, and challenges, Soviet planning. The climates are almost everywhere continental—i.e., characterized by a high seasonal range of temperature—which makes them as familiar to North Americans as they are little experienced by northwest Europeans who live under an oceanic regime. The U.S.S.R.'s territory is so vast and so withdrawn, for the most part, from the oceans that it contains many different climates enabling it to enjoy warmer summers and experience colder winters for the latitude than occur in western Europe. Actually eight types of climate can be distinguished, three of which apply to relatively small areas: (1) There is the arctic type applicable to the northernmost belt of Siberia and extending into European U.S.S.R. only in the north of the Kola Peninsula. (2) The boreal type, which applies to about one-third to one-half of the whole country, mostly to Siberia and the Far East but also to a large part of central and northern Russia. (3) and (4) The arid and semiarid climates occur over considerable areas of Middle Asia, Azerbaidzhan, and southeastern parts of European U.S.S.R. (5) The fifth type is the temperate monsoon climate, with heavy summer rains intruding only into the Maritime Territory of the Far East. (6) The marginal areas of Caucasia, especially the Black Sea coastlands of Georgia and some basins in Azerbaidzhan on the Caspian Sea, experience a subtropical climate. (7) On the southernmost coast of the Crimean Peninsula, the Mediterranean climate makes possible winter bathing and health resorts. (8) The mountain type, applicable to areas where altitude introduces rapid vertical changes of climate, occurs in Eastern Siberia, the Far East, Central Asia, the Caucasus, and elsewhere.

Table 2, which gives average annual precipitation figures and

Table 2 *Contrasting Types of Climate at Selected Stations*

Station	Location	Climatic Type	Temperature Jan. (°F.)	Temperature July (°F.)	Mean Annual Temperature Range (°F.)	Yearly Precipitation (inches)
Dudinka	Central Siberia	Arctic	−22	55	77	8.4
Novosibirsk	Western Siberia	Boreal	−2.7	65.7	68.4	14.8
Moscow	Central Russia	Boreal	15.0	65.5	50.5	24.8
Astrakhan	Lower Volga	Arid	18.5	77	58.5	6.4
Mary (Merv)	Central Asia	Arid	34	85	51	6.0
Odessa	Ukraine	Semiarid	25	72	47	14.3
Barnaul	Western Siberia	Semiarid	0	67	67	14.2
Vladivostok	Far East	Monsoon	7.3	69*	61.7	21.2
Batumi	South Caucasus	Sub-tropical	41.5	73.5*	32	95.6
Lenkoran	South Caucasus	Sub-tropical	36.5	75.5	39	49.3
Sevastopol	Crimea	Mediterranean	34.5	72	37.5	12.2

* August.

average January and July temperature figures for selected stations, suggests the principal features of these climatic types.

Among these climates the arctic and arid types present conditions which are the most hostile to human occupation and economic development. About one-tenth of the Union suffers Arctic climate, with winters of extremely low temperatures and of great length—nine to ten months—including a few months of complete darkness. The rivers and coastal waters are thus long frozen; so too the subsoil, which is covered with snow for eight or nine months. Summers are short and cool, but draw in migrant birds, especially ducks, while tree trunks drift down the open rivers. However, midges swarm to make life troublesome. The vegetation of the Arctic zone is tundra, and the lichens in particular support reindeer herds and, in scanty numbers, such primitive peoples as the Nentsy and the Chukchi. Soviet efforts to develop mineral resources and to open the short-summer sea route through the inner Arctic seas have led to the development of some small seaports, weather stations, and mining settlements for coal, oil, nickel, tin, gold, and salt. Such activities depend necessarily on the use of aircraft, as well as on water routes in summer.

Because of low rainfall, deserts and semideserts cover about one-fifth of the U.S.S.R. and lie for the most part to the east, west, and north of the Caspian Sea—in Central Asia, Kazakhstan, and the eastern side of Caucasia. Salt pans and salt deserts abound. There is a little patchy vegetation—for example, of wormwood shrubs and grasses—but the sheer desert consists of much bare stone, sand and clay, and tracts of moving sands. Summers are dry and scorching, the scanty rain falling mainly in winter. Only where rivers bring water or where canals have been cut does the cultivation of crops, by irrigation, make it practical for sedentary life. The possibility, however, of diverting southward into arid Central Asia some of the great rivers of Western Siberia (more feasible now that atomic energy is available) suggests that some part of the deserts may later on acquire real value.

To the cold and hot deserts, which are so largely negative, may be added mountainous areas offering relatively small returns: pastures and forests, notably in the Caucasus, Central Asia, south Siberia, and the Maritime Territory, but also tundra vegetation in parts of Eastern Siberia and the Far East. While mountain valleys in the more southerly latitudes give scope for cultivation and sedentary life, and also some provide mineral wealth, the mountain zones as a whole carry only low densities of population.

The boreal climatic type applies to about two-fifths of the Union's territory. This is where the taiga, forests of mainly coniferous trees, holds sway, although stretches of marsh and bog occupy about one-half of the area which is ill-drained. The northeastern half of European U.S.S.R. falls within this zone, most of which extends throughout Siberia and the Far East, with some lying south of the tundra belt of Arctic climate. Here again climate is very limiting to human occupancy. Forests of spruce, pine, and fir (but also of larch) extend widely, but they are shallow rooted where permafrost occurs, which is mainly in Eastern Siberia. The soils are acid —podzols, so-called—and the growing season is short. Winter is hard and long, its length and severity increasing northeastward. While most of the precipitation, which tends to be low, is summer rain, snow falls to cover the land for seven to ten months. At this time the rivers, which provide the main means of penetration into the forests, are frozen hard. A more congenial feature is the relative lack of cloud and wind so that sunshine is effective.

This large fraction of the Union's territory was famous for its fur-bearing animals—the sable, bear, beaver, fox, and marten—but centuries of fur hunting have depleted this resource. Forest industries, too, are naturally important in this zone, but more so in European U.S.S.R. and Western Siberia than elsewhere. The governing factors here are accessibility and the availability of water transport. Among the Union's mineral resources, diamonds, gold, platinum, tin, and coal are found within this zone. Some old Russian towns stand within or near the margins of the taiga— Leningrad, Vologda, Archangel, Perm, Tomsk, Irkutsk, and Yakutsk, for example—and this is essentially an area in which

Russians above all have long made their homes. In European U.S.S.R., on and beyond its western margin, the boreal climate loses some of its winter severity and rainfall is more adequate. Also, in the region around Moscow, it was possible over the centuries to clear much of the forest, which was of mixed coniferous and deciduous species, for settlement and agriculture. For historical reasons, economic activity, urbanization, and dense population are well marked in this part of Russia proper.

Outstanding, too, among the climatic zones of the U.S.S.R. is that which is here distinguished as semiarid. Although this accounts for only a modest fraction of the total territory—around 10 per cent—and was developed relatively late, it is beyond a doubt the most important single climatic (and vegetation) zone of the Union. It extends as a broad but tapering belt, several hundred miles wide, from western Ukraine, Moldavia, and North Caucasus eastward across the Middle Volga, Western Siberia, and northern Kazakhstan; thereafter, in the south of Eastern Siberia, it occurs discontinuously. Its northern part was naturally wooded steppe, lying south of the mixed forests of central Russia and the birch forests of Western Siberia. Southward, as the rainfall decreases, tree growth is restricted to the valleys and the feather-grass steppe (now virtually replaced by plowlands) spread everywhere. On the wooded steppe developed the deep black-earth soils, famous for their high humus content, while in the drier, treeless steppe the chestnut soils are also, but somewhat less, rewarding. In these semiarid lowlands, where the annual rainfall (mainly in summer) averages at most up to 24 inches in the extreme west and as little as 8 to 16 inches over the greater part, the U.S.S.R. finds its principal agricultural lands and also its two chief coal fields and many of its principal mineral deposits. Some parts are already well settled—for instance, the Ukraine—while other parts, notably in Western Siberia and northern Kazakhstan, show rapid population growth.

Two climatic types, which occur with only limited extent, are important in that they permit the diversification of the U.S.S.R.'s domestic resources. Because of the temperate monsoon climate in the Maritime Territory, this possesses valuable stands of hardwood trees. And the humid subtropical climate of coastal Georgia and of the Lenkoran lowland of eastern Azerbaidzhan enables the U.S.S.R. to grow crops that rarely grow elsewhere—especially tea, citrus fruits, and rice.

While climate has done much to diversify the major environments of the U.S.S.R., especially because of its role in determining soil patterns and vegetation cover, land forms and relief provide other principal differentials. The greater part of the country is lowland which extends on both sides of the Ural Mountains—in European U.S.S.R., in Middle Asia, and in Western Siberia as far east as the Yenisei River. Mountain ranges, though widely developed in Eastern Siberia, tend to lie marginally, as do the Carpathians in eastern Ukraine and Moldavia, the Caucasus, the Central Asian system, and many mountain ranges of southern Siberia. It is helpful as broad background to characterize the main units, themselves of great scale, of which the Union is composed.

THE GREAT RUSSIAN LOWLAND

The Great Russian lowland makes up the most populous region of the U.S.S.R. and includes areas significant in Russian history (see Chapter 3). It lies mainly below 600 feet, but contains hill masses rising towards 1,000 feet at the most. These continue, although much more broadly, the north European lowland and rest on a foundation of ancient crystalline rocks—the so-called Great Russian Platform. This is masked almost everywhere by young deposits, such as glacial over the northeastern half and loess to the southwest. The old rocks of the floor appear at the surface in Kola (as the Khibiny Mountains) in Karelia, and in the southwest as the Azov-Podolian Heights and the Donetz Heights in the Ukraine. Some rivers, too, have cut down their beds to expose the ancient crystalline floor, as does the Dnieper at its rapids just above Zaporozhe. Glacial action over the northeastern half of the lowlands accounts for numerous surface features—morainic masses such as the Valdai Heights from which the Volga takes its source, lake basins, expanses of boulder clay, and such ill-drained depressions as the Pripet marshes which lie within Byelorussia S.S.R. In the southwest, it is on the thick deposits of loess, which suffers much from gulleying, that the best soils of the Union have developed. The system of rivers drains northward and southward to the many seas and, thanks to the low relief, river navigation, aided by easy portages, has been available throughout Russian history. The peripheral mountains offer sharp contrasts. The Urals are worn-down mountains, which, while rising to about 10,000 feet, are in no sense a physical barrier; they are remarkably rich in metals and other minerals, and on their southwestern side are flanked by the U.S.S.R.'s richest oil field. The Caucasus, in contrast, are mountains of the Alpine type, young and high (their peaks are around 18,500 feet), and can be crossed only with difficulty at a few points. The Carpathians, although of similar age to the Caucasus, are much less high and scenic and accordingly offer more scope for pastoral and forest industries.

The European lowland, including its Ural and Caucasian borderlands, comprises many distinctive large-scale regions, which are distinguished and delimited by Soviet geographers on either political, environmental, or locational ground. Therefore in European U.S.S.R. the three Baltic republics of Estonia, Latvia, and Lithuania, together with Byelorussia, Moldavia, and the Ukraine, form politico-geographical units. In addition, distinguished broadly on locational ground, and for this reason distinctively characterized by climate and agricultural importance, there are eight regions, all of which lie within the giant republic, the R.S.F.S.R.: (1) the European northwest, with Leningrad as its major focus, together with Karelia and Kola; (2) the European northeast, which includes the Pechora basin, with some coal and oil resources, and the old seaport of Archangel; (3) the western European part of the R.S.F.S.R., which adjoins Byelorussia to the west; (4) the central industrial region, which contains Moscow, its ring of satellite towns, and many other important industrial centers; (5) the central black-earth region, to the south of this, where agriculture does well; (6)

the Volga region, which is most developed on the higher and wetter western side of the river, with many large towns and substantial agricultural resources; (7) the Lower Don and North Caucasus region, which yields coal, oil, and crop produce; and (8) the Ural industrial region, established astride the southern part of these mountains, which is notable for its deposits of iron, nonferrous metals, nonmetallic minerals, and for iron and steel and related heavy industries. Yet another region, small in scale and detached from the main body of the R.S.F.S.R., is the Kaliningrad region, the part of German East Prussia annexed to the U.S.S.R. after World War II.

SOUTH CAUCASUS (TRANSCAUCASIA)

Soviet territories in South Caucasus, situated between the Black and Caspian Seas, consist mainly of mountainous and highland country and adjoin Iran (Persia) and Turkey. Lowlands along the Caspian coast and within the Kura basin in Azerbaidzhan are dry. They are outliers of the arid country of Central Asia across the Caspian, although the Lenkoran lowland has a humid subtropical climate. The Black Sea lowlands of Georgia receive a very high rainfall, mainly in winter, and enjoy mild winters. South Caucasus is remarkable for the many peoples who have entered and stayed there, so that it houses many old established nationalities and cultures. Chief of these are the Georgians, Armenians, and Azerbaidzhanians. As a whole, the region is important for its minerals— petroleum, manganese, ferroalloys, copper, and some coal and iron. Agriculturally, it is noted for its wines, citrus fruits, tea, rice, wool, raw silk, and some cotton. Pastoral farming and lumbering penetrate the mountains. And hydroelectric power (especially in Armenia), which uses Lake Sevan as a large natural reservoir, is already available and can be considerably increased.

THE WEST SIBERIAN BASIN

This vast lowland, which lies lower than the great Russian lowlands, extends northward from the Kazakhstan hills and the

Tarbagatai Mountains to the Kara Sea, and eastward from the foot of the Urals to the River Yenisei. It is an area of glacial deposition, mainly covered by forests and marshes, with only a gentle gradient northward. Mighty rivers of the Ob-Irtysh system make their way slowly northward, and the Ob itself delivers its waters to the Kara Sea by way of the Gulf of Ob which penetrates into the lowland for about 600 miles. In the south, at and below latitude 55°N., beyond the forest edge, the lowland rises gradually into the broad belt of grass steppe. It is here that settlement, both urban and rural, has greatly expanded in this century, mostly during the Soviet period. The country continues to rise southeastward to the Kuznetsk (Kuzbas) coal basin and to the Altai plateau, of which Barnaul is the regional center, and southward into the broad hilly and mountainous zone of north Kazakhstan rich in metallic ores. In this last zone, rainfall decreases to 12 inches a year at best, announcing the approach to the extremely arid regime characteristic farther south.

THE TURANIAN BASIN [1]

This is an extensive lowland basin of internal drainage, standing above the level of the Western Siberian lowlands and suffering from severe drought. It stretches eastward from the Caspian, which provides a useful waterway for interregional transport, and contains sheer desert expanses on every side of the Aral Sea. The two principal rivers, the Amu Darya (Oxus) and the Syr Darya (Jaxtartes), draining into the Aral, permit settlement and cultivation along their courses. To the east, the arid country continues into eastern Kazakhstan where Lake Balkhash collects waters from the Ili River. Towards the desert edge in the south, the foothill belt below the Kopet Dagh and Central Asian mountains receives water from mountain-fed streams. Soviet Central Asia includes, in addition to the larger part of the Turanian basin, a share of mountains

[1] Turan, or Turanian basin, used to be called Turkestan. It is part of Central Asia, to which are added the mountain zones. Central Asia covers the four SSR's; if Kazakhstan is added, then the term "Middle Asia" should be used.

of great altitude, the higher ranges of which (for example, Tien Shan and Pamir) raise their peaks to over 20,000 feet. They carry glaciers and snow fields below the limit of perpetual snow, from which snow-melt in summer supplies water valuable to such lower ground area as the mountain-girt basin of Ferghana. The mountains themselves get a low rainfall, but they are valuable as sources of rivers, mineral wealth, and cultivable valleys and Alpine (summer) pastures. Water is clearly the dominant control of land use in the Turanian basin; saline soils occur widely, although so-called grey soils offer good agricultural possibilities if watered. Some of the rivers descending from the mountains create oases where they exhaust themselves on the plain. These oases became the sites of such old and famous cities as Merv (now Mary), Bukhara, and Samarkand.

EASTERN SIBERIA

This enormous region (2.8 million square miles) covers about one-third of the Union's territory, although it supports less than 4 per cent of its population. It extends eastward from beyond the Yenisei to beyond the Lena River. In contrast to Western Siberia, its frontage on the Arctic seas is wide; in the south, it approaches Mongolia and China. Much of the country is at plateau level, based on some of the oldest known rocks, but there are lowlands and, in the south, mountain tracts. Although summers, except in the Arctic belt, are warm, winters are very long and severe because a great part of the area is subject to permafrost. This region contains some of the longest rivers on earth—the Yenisei and the Lena are respectively 2,700 and 2,800 miles long—while the mountain-girt tectonic basin of Lake Baikal contains a lake of great depth (up to 5,710 feet) and of great area (11,580 square miles). From this lake issues the Angara River, which has rapid falls that are now being increasingly utilized for the generation of electricity.

Precipitation is mainly in summer, but, except in the south, snow covers the land for over half the year. While numerous small settled places lie within the broad zone of the taiga, where the larch is the

commonest tree, some even lie within the tundra zone, the inhabitants being concerned with lumbering, mineral working, and transport along the river route. However, the bulk of the population is concentrated in the extreme south astride the Trans-Siberian railway. Here several upland basins, with wooded steppe vegetation, have been developed for agriculture, including pastoral farming, as well as for industrial towns (Irkutsk, Chita, and Ulan Ude occupy such locations).

Eastern Siberia is outstanding for mineral wealth: gold, platinum, coal, tin, asbestos, mica, and graphite, as well as diamonds in Yakutsk, are notable resources. Hydroelectricity has very considerable potentialities, and there are coal basins beneath frozen subsoil that are yet hardly touched. Western Siberia is similar to Eastern Siberia in that it is a land of Russian colonization, although in relatively small numbers many aboriginals—for example, the Buryats and the Yakuts—survive.

THE SOVIET FAR EAST

Since this vast region lies about 5,000 miles east of Moscow, it is remote from the European U.S.S.R. Its lengthy coast exposure on the Arctic and Pacific is remarkably inhospitable, owing to the obstacles set by climate, which include a cold surface current from the Bering Strait and summer fogs, and to the generally mountainous character of the coast. The region includes the Kamchatka peninsula, which has mountains with some tundra vegetation, geothermal resources, and fishing ports. It includes, too, the island of Sakhalin, which nearly approaches the mainland, and has a regionally useful production of petroleum and coal. In the south, in relation to the Amur River and its tributary the Ussuri, settlement possibilities are relatively good and Vladivostok provides seaport and naval base facilities.

Gold, platinum, and tin workings, trapping for furs and fur farming, and lumbering industries have led to some scattering of small settlements within the mountainous northern areas which suffer extreme winters. Most of the population is grouped in the south, though, especially in towns. Sixty-nine per cent of the population is classified as urban, making this the highest figure in the whole union and a reflection of the hardships and difficulties of living in this uncongenial environment where it has so far proved impossible to grow enough grain. The sea fishery is, however, large in scale and pastoral farming relatively important. Even though primitive peoples, such as the Chukchi and the Koryaks, live in the far north, and the Jewish Autonomous Region of Birobidzhan is located in the south, immigrant Russians dominate population numbers. The Soviet Far East has always had an important place in the U.S.S.R.'s defense system for it abuts Manchuria and Korea and lies close to Japan. But for all its great extent—over a million square miles—its population density averages only four persons per square mile, despite the fact that between 1939 and 1959 its population increased by 71 per cent.

3   *The Origin and Growth of the Russian Empire*

THE U.S.S.R., like the United States, was born as a result of successful revolution. It is the successor state of the Russian Empire which grew through the centuries from the Grand Duchy of Moscow. This itself expanded by absorbing other Russian principalities and then by territorial expansion in all directions. To understand these historical processes, which form essential background to the U.S.S.R. of today, it is necessary to look back to the emergence of the Russian nation, the most numerous and remarkable of all the Slav-speaking peoples. As a prelude to this phenomenon of the later Middle Ages, we must consider the advent of the Slavs themselves.

THE EASTERN SLAVS

The Slavs are neither an ethnic group nor a nation. Indeed, they
are represented in Europe by many distinct nations—Russians,
Ukrainians, Poles, Czechs, Slovaks, Serbs, Croats, and Bulgarians,
to recall only the major groups. In the course of the last two thousand years the Slav peoples have clearly become ethnically mixed
and retained in common merely their family relationship of language. When they are first heard of fitfully during the last millennium B.C. and during the succeeding centuries of the Roman
Empire, they are often associated with others of non-Slavic tongue.
Their actual beginnings and original home are still somewhat
obscure despite attentive researches, as is indeed true in general
of all the peoples of Indo-European speech. Vernadsky[1] and others
incline to the view that the proto-Slavs were one of the many
pastoral or nomadic peoples, organized in clans and tribes, who
made their way westward along the natural route of the grass steppe
which linked Central Asia to Asia Minor (now Turkey) and to
eastern Europe. They seem to have migrated from Central Asia, with
others, during the first millennium B.C. into the steppe expanses
astride the Lower Volga. From here some moved into the Ukraine
and western Poland, while others crossed the Caucasian mountains
to reach Georgia and Asia Minor. It might thus appear that, at this
remote time, the Slavs were horsemen.

Other experts locate the earliest home of the Slavs in the Pripet
marshes, which is a large, ill-drained lowland lying on both sides
of the Pripet River, an eastward flowing tributary of the Dnieper.
Clearly, if this was an *early* home, rather than the earliest home, of
the Slavs, their Asiatic origin remains probable enough. In any case,
certain tribal Slavs, known as the Venedi, were described at the end
of the first century A.D. by the Roman writer Tacitus. They then
occupied the broad lowland of east-central Europe, wherein the
Pripet marshes are found, between East Prussia in the north and

[1] George Vernadsky, *The Origins of Russia* (Oxford: Clarendon Press,
1959).

the Galician plateau in the south, and engaged in plundering forays on foot that carried them far and fast within this zone. Other Slavs in the following century suffered defeat by the Emperor Trajan in the lower Danube region.

During the fifth and sixth centuries A.D., the Slavs dispersed widely—westward, southward, and eastward, from their homelands in east-central Europe—and it is the last movement, of the eastern Slavs so-called, that concerns us here. These Slavs slowly penetrated the wooded steppe and mixed forests of the Russian lowlands by way of its rivers and established themselves in scattered homesteads and hamlets as far east as the present Novgorod, Smolensk, and Kiev. This was a pioneering movement by relatively primitive, forest-dwelling people whose skills and economy related to shifting agriculture, game hunting, fishing, wood working and honey gathering. Although they succeeded in occupying the western part of the wooded steppe, the Slavs were unable to colonize the grass steppe to the south because of the superior strength of the mounted nomads who controlled it. The processes were begun which ultimately led to the creation of the Slav-speaking nations of the present-day U.S.S.R.—the Great Russians, Byelorussians, and Ukrainians—and to the foundation of Russian principalities from which the Russian state of Muscovy emerged. At the same time a forward frontier movement began which was to carry Russian colonists ever eastward—to the Volga and the Urals, and beyond these to the Arctic and the Pacific.

By the eighth century A.D., the eastern Slavs effectively held the wooded plains which stretched from the Baltic gulfs of Riga and Finland in the north to the northern edge of the grass steppe in the south. They were flanked on the one hand by Baltic seamen and on the other by steppe horsemen, who were immigrants from Central Asia. The Slavs' settlement distribution, lines of movement, and tribal organization depended much on the great navigable rivers and their tributary streams: the West Dvina and Volkhov in the north, the Upper Volga and Oka in the center (between which they wrested the land from earlier Finnish occupiers), and the

Dnieper in the south. Small towns grew up at carefully selected sites related to the facilities of river navigation. Examples are Novgorod on the Volkhov, the water route to the Gulf of Finland; Polotsk on the West Dvina, the route to the Gulf of Riga; Smolensk on the Upper Dnieper; and Kiev, lower down the Dnieper, near the southern edge of the wooded steppe. These towns served a variety of purposes, such as fortified places, ports, trading and industrial centers, collecting points for tribute paid in kind, and lastly as administrative capitals.

Certainly in the eighth century these Slav tribes became sufficiently organized to succeed in reopening the overland, river-and-portage routes between the Baltic Sea and both the Black and Caspian Seas. This involved some of them, notably the tribes centered in Kiev, in paying tribute to the Turkish Khazars, who controlled the grass steppe through which their water routes passed. This trade, though it became subject to the recurrent hazards of steppe horsemen, was to become lucrative. The reason is that it was directed toward two well-organized and civilized realms—the Byzantine (or East Roman) Empire, with its capital at Constantinople; and the lands of the Caliphate, with its capital in turn at Damascus and Baghdad.

THE SCANDINAVIAN INTRUSION
AND KIEVAN RUSSIA

A new phase in the social, economic, and political organization of the eastern Slavs arose from the ninth century onward with the intrusion from the Baltic of the Varangians of Sweden. These sea rovers came as warriors and traders, to some extent at least by invitation of Slavic princes, and stayed not only to trade, but also to organize and rule. The Varangian Northmen were called "the men of Rus" but, even though this appears to be the origin of the name "Russe" from which ultimately the word "Russian" is derived, it seems that "Russes" was eventually applied to both Varangian and Slav members of the population. Although the Varangians became only a substantial minority, they established themselves in the industrial and trading towns along the major rivers and assumed the leading position in trading, military, and governmental affairs. Even so, they were assimilated in time with the native population, whose Slavic speech came to prevail. A vigorous foreign trade developed by way of the rivers and the Azov, Black, and Caspian seas, in products derived from tribute in the form of slaves and forest products (furs, honey, and wax). From Constantinople, scholars introduced a Greek alphabet which was adopted by the Russes, who were converted from the same source to Greek Orthodox Christianity in the ninth and tenth centuries. Further developments, which owed much to the stimulus and energies of the Varangians, were the growth of provinces (each organizing several Slav tribes) based on the major towns, and of principalities, of which Novgorod, Smolensk, and Kiev were among the earliest and most powerful.

Between the tenth and the twelfth centuries the city of Kiev, set on the high right bank of the Dnieper, organized a mercantile state extending from the Gulf of Finland to the margin of the wooded steppe, the cohesion and trade of which depended on the use of the rivers. Even the principality of Novgorod accepted Kiev's leadership, since it needed foodstuffs and trading facilities which Kiev controlled. Kievan Russia, with a population estimated at between seven and eight million, held no permanent footholds on the southern sea coasts and suffered continually from the steppe horsemen. And although Kiev, "mother of Russia," played an important part in the development of the Russian people by deriving from Constantinople many elements of civilization, it was Moscow further north in the seclusion of its mixed forests and marshes, which was able later to forge Muscovy, the precursor of the Russian Empire.

THE BEGINNINGS OF MUSCOVY

With the decline of Kievan Russia in the second half of the twelfth century, some of its peoples moved northeastward into Suzdal, the lands between the Upper Volga and Oka rivers, to colonize and develop further this centrally placed area of the

Russian lowlands. Less congenial in climate and less agriculturally productive, this area was more defensible from external attacks and well placed for expansion in all directions by way of the rivers. These pioneers, adding to the existing population of Russians and Finns, made clearings for agriculture, developed handicrafts, set about the trapping and hunting of forest animals for their furs, and settled down in dispersed hamlets. The Orthodox (Greek) Church was established in Suzdal, and it was there too that the Great Russian people and language evolved. Although Moscow itself did not become capital until 1263, in less than a century it achieved primacy over most of the other Russian principalities.

For several centuries, however, the Russian people were beset by stronger neighbors who either conquered them outright or reduced them to vassalage. From the east and south advanced the Golden Horde from its bases on the Volga and Don rivers: for over two hundred years after 1242 A.D. these nomads, at first pagan and later Moslem, made up of Tatars and others and led by Mongols, were able to exact tribute from the Russian principalities. Moreover, to the west and southwest the Lithuanians and Poles, who formed a dynastic union in 1386, won control of an extensive territory between the Baltic and the Black seas. Indeed, Lithuania-Poland became the major Russian state, since it contained a large Russian population settled in Galicia, in Volhynia, and even in those historic Russian lands on and eastward of the Dnieper which included the cities of Smolensk and Kiev. The Grand Prince of Moscow, although himself subject to the Mongols, acquired the position of leader of the other Russian principalities. As suzerain prince of Russia, he was entrusted by the Great Khan with the collection of the Russian tribute. Moscow, too, was raised in status when it became (in 1326) the seat of the Metropolitan, the head of the Russian Church.

Meanwhile in the north, Great Novgorod had built up a vast trading empire between Lake Peipus, the West Dvina River, and the White Sea. A mixed Russian, Scandinavian, and Finnish population sought the wealth in furs of the coniferous forests and traded between the Volga and the Baltic: Novgorod itself became a depot of the Hanseatic League of commercial cities. As hunters and trappers spread ever northeastward through the forests toward and beyond the north Urals, Novgorod conquered, and drew tribute in furs from, the local scattered population. However, in 1478 Ivan III, the Grand Prince of Moscow, incorporated Novgorod's empire, thus greatly enlarging his territory and securing in the North Dvina a route to the White Sea. At about this time, in 1480, Moscow ceased to be a dependency of the Golden Horde.

THE TERRITORIAL EXPANSION OF MUSCOVY

Hemmed in to the west by the Lithuanians and Poles and to the south and east by the Horde which was part of a great Asiatic power, Muscovy could at first expand only towards the north and northeast (see Figure 5): the Russians, essentially a forest people, were thus confined to the forests. Even Novgorod's narrow outlet to the Baltic by the Gulf of Finland was closed by the Swedes who established themselves on its southern and northern sides, respectively in Ingia and Karelia. Only on the shores of the White Sea, which was frozen over and useless for nearly half the year, did Muscovy have direct access to the Atlantic and Arctic oceans—and the latter offered little scope for navigation until the technological advances of the present century. Despite a long struggle waged between 1558 and 1581, Ivan IV, the Terrible, failed to force the Swedes to yield him access to the Baltic. It was he who first assumed the title of "tsar" with all that it implied in imperialist pretensions. For tsar is derived from the Latin Caesar, and Ivan took this title because the Roman Empire had come to its final end in 1453 with the fall of Constantinople to the Ottoman Turks.

Russia moves southeast and east. When, during the latter half of the sixteenth century, Muscovy was again able to take the initiative against its enemies, success was achieved only eastward and southeastward of Moscow against the Tatar khanates which then ruled the mixed forest and steppe country toward the Volga and the Urals. The fall of Kazan on the Lower Oka in 1552 made it

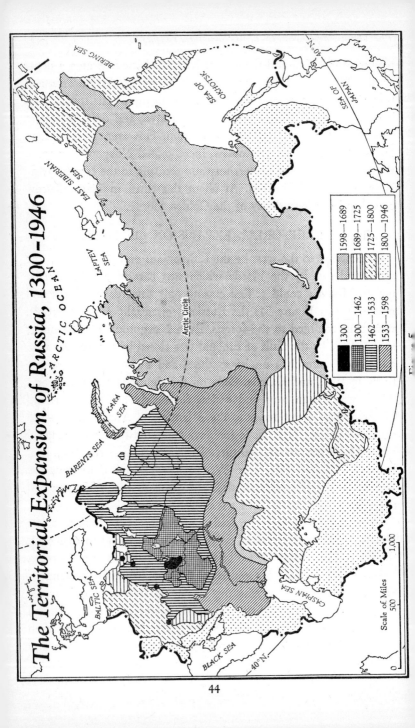

The Territorial Expansion of Russia, 1300–1946

Legend:
1598–1689
1689–1725
1725–1800
1800–1946

1300
1300–1462
1462–1533
1533–1598

BERING SEA
SEA OF OKHOTSK
SEA OF JAPAN
EAST SIBERIAN SEA
LAPTEV SEA
ARCTIC OCEAN
Arctic Circle
KARA SEA
BARENTS SEA
BALTIC SEA
BLACK SEA
CASPIAN SEA

40° N.
60° N.

Scale of Miles
0   500   1,000

44

possible for the Russians to start their great expansion which was to carry them to the Volga, the Caspian Sea, the Urals, and thence across Siberia to the Pacific. Astrakhan fell to them in 1556 and by 1581 they had crossed the central Urals. At the end of the century their great trek across the forests of Siberia was just beginning, and by the 1640's they had set up posts on the far Pacific. Their conquests were made against dispersed and seminomadic tribes, and by the use of rivers and their portages at ever-increasing distances from their base. Fortified settlements were established, among which may be noted those at Tobolsk on the Middle Irtysh in 1587, at Yeniseisk on the Yenisei in 1618, at Yakutsk on the Lena in 1630, and at Okhotsk on the Pacific coast in 1647.

A forest people lured on by the lucrative trade in furs (these were exacted as tribute from the local population), the Russians thus acquired early a vast colonial territory, with only a scanty population, yet containing great sources of wealth which are only now being continually revealed. It is of interest that they reached their third sea—Okhotsk—long before they did the European waters of the Baltic, Azov, and Black seas. The remote Pacific ports, closed by ice for more than half the year, offered them little scope for about a century. Archangel, founded in 1585, became their only direct gateway to the ocean: the English seaman Richard Chancellor, by sailing into the White Sea in 1553, had forged a trade link by sea between Muscovy and England. The Russians, too, so far from home in their far east, were not strong enough to hold the best lands for agriculture and settlement—those astride the lower Amur River—where Chinese peasants, under strong Manchu rule, held them at bay. Also, it should be noted that the Russians were unable, until the eighteenth century, to expand southward from the Siberian forests, into the nomad's world of the steppe, since Tatar-Mongol power persisted there.

Russia reaches the Baltic. When Peter the Great was born (1672), as indeed when he assumed personal rule in 1696, Russia appeared a vast Asiatic state, turned away from Europe and shut off by hostile powers from the Baltic, Azov, and Black seas. Its detachment from Europe owed much to the external influences to which it had long been subject—on the one hand from Constantinople, and on the other, from the Golden Horde. Indeed, during the three centuries before Peter the Great, Russia had been cut off from the effects of those great cultural movements which had revolutionized life and thought in Europe: the Renaissance, the Reformation, the geographical discoveries, and the beginnings of modern science. As it stood territorially, Russia fell far short of the areas of Russian settlement. Its western boundary reached the Lower Dnieper, the historic river of the Russian people, but not the whole of its course; only in 1667 were Smolensk and Kiev recovered, together with left-bank (eastern) Ukraine.

A great stretch of country to the west of the Dnieper, including the Pripet marshlands, Galicia, and Volhynia, was largely settled by Russian peasants, though ruled by Polish or Lithuanian landowners within the Lithuanian-Polish kingdom. These Russians had acquired cultural traits which distinguished them from the people of Muscovy. Byelorussian (White Russian) and Ukrainian speech had developed and were to be recognized later (in the nineteenth century) as Slav languages in their own right. Many of the Russians under Polish-Lithuanian rule had, since 1596, become members of the Uniate Church, in which, while Orthodox liturgy and rites were retained, the Pope was accepted as head. This deviation clearly owed much to the influence of their Polish and Lithuanian masters who were Roman Catholics.

As to the west, so to the south and north, Muscovy was subjected to strong extraneous pressures. The Ottoman Turks, successors to the Byzantine Empire, extended their Moslem rule to the Crimea and the neighboring coasts of the Black Sea which they monopolized. And to the north, in the Baltic lands, either Germans or Swedes held sway over the local populations of Finns, Estonians, and Letts (Latvians). There, under western influences, the Lutheran faith prevailed and economic life was more vigorous and advanced than in Muscovy.

During the lifetime of Peter the Great (1672-1725), Russia, relatively secure on its Asiatic flank, successfully challenged its enemies in Europe and ceased to be merely an Asiatic and largely landlocked state. Indeed, by 1721, it had emerged as one of the great powers of Europe. Peter himself, strong and ruthless, combined an interest in military and naval affairs with a down-to-earth concern with, and aptitude for, craftsmanship and economic affairs. He sensed that his countrymen could learn much of practical value from western Europe, which he visited on many occasions, and adopted the policy of enlisting westerners in his service. Thus he stimulated such industries as iron and copper working in the Urals, shipbuilding, engineering, and armaments manufacturing and encouraged trade with the West. To this end he was astute enough to break the girdle of his enemies by making an alliance with Poland, so that he could better wage war against the Turks and the Swedes. Although he could not drive the Turks from the Azov-Black seas, he at least kept them from the Caspian. In the north, he fought the Swedes unremittingly between 1700 and 1721, when he achieved complete success. The Baltic lands of Karelia, Ingria, Estonia, and Livonia passed into his hands—and for a time Finland, too. Already in 1703 he had begun the building of his new capital at St. Petersburg which was to open his window to the West, become the largest city of the world at such northerly latitudes, and remain Russia's capital until 1918. Not only did Peter create a powerful army and fleet which came to dominate the Baltic, but also he reorganized the finances, created a bureaucracy, and centralized the government under his own autocratic control from his new capital.

Russia expands to the west, north, and south. Given the nature of the Great Russian lowland and the fact that many Russians remained under Polish rule, it is not surprising that Russia sought to expand westward during the century which followed the death of Peter the Great in 1725. The Lowland set no clear physical limits to the territories of this strong nation, so that independence and security there could only be sought by a forward policy, for which Peter bequeathed both the means and the method. The situation had changed sharply from the days when (in 1610) the Poles took

Moscow and installed a tsar; rather the tsars interfered continually in Polish affairs so as to ensure the political weakness of Poland. The outcome of Poland's internal weakness in the eighteenth century was its partition between Russia, Austria, and Prussia and its effacement from the map of Europe. Russia thus made large territorial gains which advanced its limits 300 miles westward into east-central Europe—to the Niemen, the headwaters of the Pripet, and the Dniester. To the lands which Russia acquired by the first and second partitions of 1772 and 1793 respectively, it had reasonable claims in that they contained a majority of either White Russians or Ukrainians, and were naturally regarded as Russia's western lands. But for those won by the third partition of 1795 there was no justification, since their population was mainly Polish and Lithuanian. The effacement of Poland only created a legacy of problems, for the Polish nation survived to aspire to independent statehood. This was satisfied in modified form when in 1809 Napoleon set up the Grand Duchy of Warsaw, but only in token form when a small Polish kingdom—with the tsar as king—was created in 1815 at the Congress of Vienna. This expedient, which reduced Poland to the status of a Russian dependency, was to last, however, until the resettlement of Europe after World War I.

Russian expansion in the north was a result of its last wars with Sweden, which ended in 1809 with the conquest of Finland, and its incorporation into the Russian Empire as a Grand Duchy possessing its own constitution, laws, and tariffs. This acquisition was considered necessary to safeguard St. Petersburg from external attack, and it also strengthened Russia's position in the Baltic Sea.

It was towards the south that Russia's expansion was more remarkable during the last two hundred years of the Russian Empire. For centuries Russia had been contained within its mixed forests by the occupants of the steppe, mainly Tatars who owed vassalage to the Turkish Empire. Seven wars were fought with Turkey between 1676 and 1812 before the New Russia of the steppe could be possessed for peasant colonization and the shores of the Azov and Black seas acquired for navigation and trade. This great achievement was mainly that of the Empress Catherine II (The Great). But much credit can be given to the hosts of Cossack horsemen, who were Orthodox Christians with a free hand to encroach on the grass steppe, as well as to the steady advance of Russian and Ukrainian colonists into its northern wooded margin. By 1812 the empire included the whole Black Sea coast, together with the Crimean peninsula, from the Prut River and the Danube delta to the Caucasus. Already Catherine had wrested from the Turks in 1774 the right for Russian merchant ships to navigate within the Black Sea and to pass through the Turkish straits en route to the Mediterranean: this was the first breach in the Turkish monopoly of the Black Sea waters and it took many years to consolidate.

On two of its Asiatic borders Russia made striking advances: beyond the Urals in Western Siberia, Kazakhstan, and Central Asia; and beyond the Caucasus on the confines of Persia and Turkey. In Western Siberia Russian pressure was directed southward from the coniferous forests into the belt of mixed forests and thence into the grass steppe. Omsk in the former belt was settled in 1716, and Semipalatinsk, in the latter, two years later. Then began, slowly at first, Russian colonization of these relatively favored agricultural zones, beyond the fur-rich forests which had lured them first. Expansion southward, once started, continued and by stages brought the Altai plateau and the Kazakhstan steppes and deserts into Russian hands.

Beyond the Caucasus, by conquests and cessions between 1801 and 1829, the empire incorporated from Turkey and Persia an outer bastion for defense which included many peoples of an ancient civilization—the Georgians, Armenians, and Azerbaidzhani being the most numerous—each distinct in language, religion, and cultural traditions. Also, the empire acquired an extension of its Caspian front plus the rich oil resources of Baku, which Peter the Great had temporarily held. From Caspian ports Russia was able, between 1864 and 1885, to launch successful military campaigns against the Tatar khanates of Central Asia: the advance from Lake Aral had proved too difficult because of the sheer distances and of desert

expanses. The conquest in Central Asia added substantial populations of Sunni Moslems, and yet other national groups with their
distinctive cultures: the Turkmen, the Uzbeks, the Kirghiz, the
Tadzhiks, and many more of smaller scale. Russia sought to bind
these regions, remote from the old centers of Muscovy, by railroad
construction of the Transcaspian (1888) and Central Asian (1905)
lines. Similarly, the Trans-Siberian railway, completed in 1903, and
the line to Baku, made possible the administration and retention of
its dependencies and the development of trade. By these many accessions the multinational character of the Russian Empire was greatly
enhanced.

The last of Russia's southerly advances was in the Far East, where
since the Treaty of Nerchinsk in 1689—the first Sino-Russian treaty
ever made—China had successfully held the Russians back from
the lower Amur lands (Russia acquired them in 1860, however).
Vladivostok, "Guardian of the East," which was to become the
terminus of the Trans-Siberian railroad, was founded to command
the fine harbor in St. Peter's Bay.

4   *The Soviet Union: Its Advent and Political Organization*

THE transformation of the Russian Empire into the
Union of Soviet Socialist Republics was one of the unexpected
results of World War I. Like the German, Austro-Hungarian, and
Turkish empires, it foundered under the dual strain of war and
defeat. Unlike these others, however, it was replaced by a state
which, with all its revolutionary novelty, became another empire
in all but name. It is very clear that the collapse of the Russian
Empire—which could not stay the course until the war was won—

presented the opportunity for revolutionary change. But it is less evident, in the light of its apparent strength and of its historic endurance, why imperial Russia collapsed.

THE END OF THE RUSSIAN EMPIRE

The Russian Empire had long figured as a great power backed by one of the largest populations in the world—about 130 million in 1897—and renowned for its apparent toughness, vigor, and political resilience. It occupied a vast territory, larger than that which the U.S.S.R. has attained, and one which projected further to the west than does the U.S.S.R. today. Its economy showed elements of strength. Large agricultural surpluses were available for export, and its enormous peasant population had been freed from serfdom since 1861. Industrialization, though late to start, had made headway during the half century before World War I, thanks largely to foreign capital and enterprise, especially from France, Germany, and Britain. Its railway system, if skeletal by west European standards, linked together its many provinces and provided access to ports on many seas. Its system of government depended on an autocratic tsar, who ruled by divine right, and was supported by a state church (which on occasions disclosed the secrets of the confessional), a large bureaucracy, and a vigilant corps of secret police. Tsardom as such was not impugned, although new forces had long been shaping which sought to effect major social and political changes. A widespread revolution in 1905-1906, which followed Russia's defeat by Japan; and the constitution won in 1906, which permitted members elected on a very narrow franchise to sit in the state Duma (parliament)—these did not really challenge a regime which defended the few "haves" from the many "have-nots."

The Russian government was signally unprepared for World War I, and the Russian masses had no idea why it was being fought. Had the war proved short and successful, the Russian Empire might have been offered a brief respite, but fundamental changes in the social, economic, and political system were long overdue. As it was, the continuance of the war served only to aggravate Russia's serious internal weakness: a loose-limbed giant, it was vulnerable not only from the enemy without but also from disruptive forces within. Above all, it lacked social homogeneity and cohesion, as it lacked too what is now called the "state-idea," that is, a realization by its peoples of a distinctive and acceptable *raison d'être*. Not only was the population markedly multinational, though subjected to a policy of Russification, but it was sharply divided into the very few educated and the largely illiterate masses. The latter consisted of the peasants, who made up 80 per cent of the empire's population. Although—or perhaps because—their low living standards had risen somewhat during the war, they were aggrieved and restive for various immediate and long-term reasons: the losses of their fellow countrymen in battle, the high cost of living and the shortage of industrial goods, an unfair tax burden, the smallness of their holdings, and their desire to appropriate lands from the well-off peasants and the large estates. In the towns the factory workers, numbering several millions, had shown their patriotism by cooperating with the government through their representatives on the War Industries Committees. But, as living conditions worsened, they increasingly turned to trade union activities, including strikes, and by 1917 were seeking to obtain control of the factories. In the armed forces, to which 15 million men had been called, lack of munitions and supplies, the evident superiority of enemy forces, and hopeless mismanagement and leadership induced apathy, wholesale desertions to the enemy, and a longing for peace at any price. The situation was so critical that the army was disintegrating before the first revolution took place in Petrograd in February-March 1917. Moreover, the administration of the country, divided from the start of the war between the High Command and the civilian authorities, proved wholly inadequate to its heavy tasks.

An additional misfortune for Russia was that Nicholas II wholly lacked the high abilities needed during such a grave and prolonged emergency. By assuming direct command of his armies in the field, he inevitably incurred direct responsibility for their defeat. The tsarina, left to rule in the capital, which took the name Petrograd in 1914, fell under the sway of the charlatan and debauchee, Rasputin, and failed miserably to secure an effective council of ministers. Further, since Russia was beset by many enemies—Germany, Austro-Hungary, and Turkey—all her western ports except Murmansk and Archangel were inaccessible to her allies. Thus catastrophe was imminent before the first disorders occurred in the capital in February-March 1917, although these were a spontaneous outbreak which surprised both liberal and revolutionary circles.

This outbreak, in which the Petrograd garrison joined the factory workers, brought about the abdication of the tsar and the formation of a short-lived provisional government that was middle class and liberal in character. During the succeeding months this government found itself powerless to curb the rising tide of revolutionary feeling both in the countryside and in the towns. The government's policy, which aimed at prosecuting the war to a successful conclusion and at summoning a constituent assembly to determine a constitution for Russia, proved neither practicable nor desirable at a time when *soviets* (councils) of factory workers, peasants, soldiers, and sailors were springing up all over the country, adopting revolutionary slogans, and taking direct action. The real revolutionaries, who had long been working underground in Russia and abroad—unless they were living under restraint in Siberia—played only a minor part in the first revolution. But Lenin in exile, who combined a profound knowledge of conditions in Russia with a strong belief in the applicability to his country of the socialist doctrines of Karl Marx, was preparing for a revolution. Carried out by the working masses in town and country, it would overthrow the existing state, church, and economic and social orders. His aims conflicted with those of the right wing of his party, which looked for support to the intellectuals and the bourgeoisie and which, seeking only limited objectives, was willing to compromise with the regime.

In Lenin, Russia found an experienced, gifted, and humane leader who knew how to organize his followers and knew also what good organization could achieve. Under his leadership the majority of the revolutionaries became known, after 1903, as the Bolsheviks: the word meant "majority," just as Menshevik meant "minority" (the group which sought to avoid an all-out collision with tsardom). After the arrival of Lenin in Petrograd on April 4, 1917, and of Trotsky a month later, the Bolsheviks were able to win control of the Petrograd soviet, to which delegates were being sent from the provinces. Although, as Trotsky put it, "hardly more than a banner —with no printing works, no funds, no branches,"[1] the Bolsheviks suited the mood of the factory workers, the poorer peasants, and the servicemen by their understandable call to end the war, launch a class struggle, and divide up among the poorer peasants the larger farms and big estates. In October 1917 the Bolsheviks easily overthrew the provisional government which was powerless to resist, for the administration, the armed forces, and the economy of the country had collapsed. The Bolsheviks were as surprised as elated at their quick seizure of power and unsure whether they could consolidate it. Certainly they faced enormous difficulties for several years, although they had a corps of trained leaders and had roughly outlined their policy. They had, as Lenin believed, enabled the poor and oppressed to triumph over the great and the powerful; they had "abolished a régime of despair and created a new world of hope."[2]

THE FORMATION OF THE SOVIET UNION

In their triumph the Bolshevik leaders were at once confronted by grave and mounting difficulties of many kinds. Russia was still at war, German forces were penetrating deeply into its western borderlands, and the Turks were pressing on the South Caucasus border. In fear of a German assault on Petrograd, which was renamed Leningrad in 1924 on the death of Lenin, they moved the capital to Moscow and set about ending the so-called imperialist war, almost regardless of the terms offered them. This was accomplished by the

[1] Cited by M. T. Florinsky, *The End of the Russian Empire* (New York: Collier Books, 1961), p. 244.

[2] Christopher Hill, *Lenin and the Russian Revolution* (London: Houghton and Stoughton Ltd., 1947), Chap. VIII.

Treaty of Brest-Litovsk in March 1918. Their allies, alarmed at Russia's defection and more alarmed at the unleashing of revolutionary forces which were spreading outside Russia, attempted to rally antirevolutionary "White" opposition by landing troops and supplies. British, Japanese, and American forces established themselves at Vladivostok and British troops landed at Archangel and also entered Russia through Persia. Three years of destruction and misery over wide areas of the country followed. Allied intervention won little support locally and failed completely in its attempt to stamp out Bolshevism at its source, even if, by diverting Bolshevik energies, it checked the spread of revolutionary ideas and activities beyond Russia's western borders.[3]

The new regime faced its first and sternest test—and survived. At the end of 1918, the direct control of the Soviet government was restricted to the modest area of Muscovy in the sixteenth century. During 1919 Admiral Kolchak's mixed Allied and Russian forces advanced from Siberia across the Urals. General Denikin, with British and French support, moving up from the south, reached Kiev, Orel, and the Volga above Tsaritsin.[4] The worst crisis of this war had been passed in August 1918 when Denikin's army threatened Moscow. The Bolsheviks succeeded in weathering these storms because they were strong in their appeal to the masses, notably in promising the poorer peasants a free hand to share in the land, the machinery, and the livestock. Had the Whites with Allied support triumphed, it was widely believed that the landlords would have returned and, with them, Great Russian predominance and oppression. Trained members of the Bolshevik Party were few in number for the tasks which beset them. Although councils of workers and peasants were active everywhere, support for its rivals, the Mensheviks, as in Georgia, remained strong. The interventionist war, together with the inevitable difficulties of such a complete transition,

[3] For detailed discussion of this period, see George Kennan, *Russia and the West under Lenin and Stalin* (Boston: Little, Brown & Co., 1961).

[4] Tsaritsin was renamed Stalingrad in honor of Stalin, who was alleged to have taken a prominent part in its defense during the civil war.

reduced Russia to its lowest ebb. Crop yields fell to less than half the pre-World War I level; heavy and consumer industries were greatly stricken; internal transport and trade broke down; and the country was blockaded from outside. Only in 1921, after immeasurable human suffering and an end to war, which for Russia had lasted seven years, could Lenin turn his attention to economic and political reorganization.

Lenin's nationality policy. The Russian Empire, like Europe itself, was an association of many nations sharply different in scale, history, and levels of culture. To the Bolshevik leaders, nations appeared awkward survivals from the past. Furthermore, they represented interests and attitudes which competed with those which the party held fundamental, the more so since their emotional appeal was international. The problem was how political control by the proletariat, in its own interests, could be won and safeguarded against bourgeois, potentially separatist, national interests. How, too, could the revolutionary movement, which sought to enlist the cooperation of workers in town and country everywhere regardless of nationality, hope to flourish when, as during World War I, workers, peasants, and allegedly revolutionary parties outside Russia had put national interests first—national interests which were much involved in imperialism?

Although Stalin himself, at Lenin's suggestion, published as early as 1913 a study of the nationality problem, *Marxism and the National Question,* his work has been rated pedestrian; it was Lenin who devised the basic principles of policy which in fact proved highly successful. Lenin recognized that nations were obstinate realities, with specific locations, languages, cultures, and standpoints which could not be either easily or quickly eliminated. Wide areas of Russia's borderlands were occupied by nations which had suffered oppression under the rule of governor-generals appointed by the tsar: in Poland, the Ukraine, South Caucasus, Middle Asia, and elsewhere. Lenin's policy was to try to win the support of national groups and, so far as was possible, to lead them towards the goals of policy under the centralized control of the party leaders in Moscow.

But if this assimilation seemed impossible, he was willing to offer national self-determination, including the right of secession. He did not wish to establish a federal organization of the country that would weaken the political control of the Bolsheviks and prevent their carrying out their program of fundamental change.

In any event, owing to the advances of the German armies, the Bolsheviks had no other choice than to accept, by the Treaty of Brest-Litovsk, the loss of Finland, Estonia, Latvia, and Lithuania, which proclaimed their political independence as republics. Moreover, the Bolsheviks lost Russia's Polish territory, since the Republic of Poland was re-created; they lost, also to Poland, western lands which were largely Russian and Ukrainian in settlement when the Poles, without authority from the western Allies, overran these lands in 1919. Other territorial losses that they had to accept included Bessarabia, which reverted to the kingdom of Rumania; the provinces of Kars and Ardahan, which were assigned to Turkey; and the southern part of Sakhalin Island in the Far East, which (as Karafuto) passed to Japan. Later, in the early 1930's, as Japanese power increased in the Far East, the U.S.S.R. renounced the formerly imperialist interests in Manchuria inherited from the Russian Empire. In short, the territorial base which came to be organized as the U.S.S.R. was considerably restricted, but at least it was unembarrassed by the nationalities which were least attracted to its political creed.

The forging of the Union of Soviet Socialist Republics. At the beginning of 1918, Russia as a viable political entity scarcely existed, but by the end of 1922 the U.S.S.R. had emerged with control over the bulk of the territories of imperial Russia. This remarkable achievement was due to the success of the Communist leaders in Moscow, notably the Bolshevik left wing, in integrating the remaining non-Russian peoples of their borderlands. A Commissariat of Nationality Affairs, with Stalin in charge, was set up in November 1917 and it was agreed, with some reluctance, that the state should be based on the novel principle of national-territorial autonomy. Even so, Lenin's enlightened policy on the nationality problem underwent considerable modification in its application to the national movements which sprang up on all sides—in Ukraine and Byelorussia, in Transcaucasus, among the Tatars of Crimea and the Volga-Urals, and in Central Asia.

Fortunately for the party leaders the many national movements suffered from divergent objectives, ineffective leadership, and political immaturity. Allied intervention, with its indifference to regional national sentiment and hope to restore prerevolution conditions, also favored the Bolsheviks who offered cultural liberties together with association in a socialized Russia—and all the proletarian gains promised by the revolution. But while they worked with national leaders and proselytized national socialism, the Bolsheviks had no intention of allowing national selfdetermination to become either a cloak to counterrevolution or a means of weakening centralized control. They had certain strong cards: they knew their objectives, they controlled units of the Red army, and they offered a new deal, which had to be accepted. Moreover, Great Russian chauvinism, to Lenin's personal dismay, figured strikingly in the ruthless Soviet strategy. The Bolsheviks, heirs to the tsars, had every intention of preserving as much as possible of Russia and of ruling it as a centralized state, albeit federal in form, so that their revolutionary purposes could be achieved. In the long, drawn-out process whereby Moscow won control of, and integrated, the borderland nations, while much depended on the activities of regional party groups and on skilled diplomacy, it would appear that the decisive fact always was the eventual entry of Red Army units: indeed, the U.S.S.R. represents the integration of conquered territories into one state.

It is understandable that, when in December 1922 the new Russia first took political shape as the union of Soviet Socialist Republics, it consisted of those considerable areas of the old Russia where Slav-speaking nations were concentrated. The three founding members of the federated U.S.S.R. were the Russian Soviet Federative Socialist Republic and the Ukrainian and the Byelorussian Soviet Socialist Republics. The first clearly dominated in population numbers, territory, and resources and comprised the bulk of the Great Russians. However, it did contain also many national groups, such as the Moslem Tatars and Bashkirs and the Christian Chuvash, Mari, and Votiak of the Volga-Ural area, and the Crimean Tatars, each of which had been accorded a very modest measure of self-government in this so-called federation. Byelorussia, on the western flank of the R.S.F.S.R., contained only that half of the White Russian nation which, by the Treaty of Riga (March 21, 1919), had escaped absorption by Poland. The Ukraine, cheated of the complete independence sought by some of its national leaders and territorially reduced by Polish acquisitions, brought to the U.S.S.R. promise of its great wealth of foodstuffs, coal, and ores. As it was constituted at the start of its career, the U.S.S.R. was smaller than imperial Russia. Nevertheless, it had the economic sinews of a strong and viable state for, in addition to the potential of the Ukraine, it held the industrial regions of Moscow, Petrograd, and the Urals, as well as the whole of Siberia and the steppes of Kazakhstan.

Some years elapsed before the Asiatic borderlands of Central Asia and South Caucasus were organized into soviet socialist republics on the basis of their national cultures and admitted as full members of the Union. The Uzbek S.S.R. and the Turkmen S.S.R. joined in 1925; the Tadzhik S.S.R. followed in 1929; and in 1936 outlying Middle Asian areas of the U.S.S.R. were formed into the Kazakh and Kirghiz S.S.R.s. In the same year the nations of South Caucasus, who had survived the intervention of German, Turkish, and Allied forces and had formed the Transcaucasian Soviet Federative Socialist Republic, broke up into the three national republics of Georgia, Armenia, and Azerbaidzhan and became full members of the U.S.S.R. Not until 1940 during World War II, when the U.S.S.R. was co-operating uneasily with Nazi Germany but was already expanding westward, did the membership of the Union increase from 11 to 16. The new accessions were the Baltic republics of Estonia, Latvia, and Lithuania, whose independent statehoods were ended when they were occupied by the Red Army; the Karelo-Finnish S.S.R., which stood on the Soviet border of Finland; and the Moldavia S.S.R., which abutted Rumania and the southwest

Ukraine. These last two had been earlier created at a lower administrative level with an eye respectively on neighboring Finnish and Rumanian territory, which indeed were later acquired (see Table 3, p. 61). The number of Union republics fell to 15 in 1956, since the Karelo-Finnish S.S.R. was then downgraded as the Karelian A.S.S.R. (Autonomous Soviet Socialist Republic), and as such became part of the R.S.F.S.R.: it had served its purpose as a means of territorial expansion at the expense of Finland.

THE POLITICAL-TERRITORIAL PATTERNS
OF THE U.S.S.R.

In form, the federal structure of the Soviet Union differs sharply from the unitary structure of the Russian Empire, although in practice much remained the same, notably the continuance of centralized rule from the capital and the predominance of the Great Russians. The difference was that for the tsar, his ministers, and his bureaucratic system were substituted Stalin, the Party leaders, and the Party. The administrative patterns of tsarist Russia were, however, completely transformed, and they continue in some measure to change in relation to two principles: nationality and administrative efficiency.

The Soviet leaders made innovations when they adopted the national-territorial principle as the basis for the component states of their federation. Here they were forced to recognize that many national groups were sufficiently localized, homogeneous, culturally advanced, and self-conscious to require at the least cultural autonomy. They all have a minimum of one million inhabitants and, since they enjoy under the 1936 constitution the right to secede from the Union, they each possess a boundary with at least one foreign state. Table 3 suggests how greatly they vary in scale, location, language, and manpower (see also Figure 6).

Numerous other national groups made similar, if less substantial, claims to political recognition. Twenty of these are organized at the lower level of the A.S.S.R.'s (Autonomous Soviet Socialist Republics), which are subordinated to the governments of Union republics.

TABLE 5 *The Constituent Republics of the U.S.S.R.*

Name	Date of Incorporation	Area (sq. mi.)	Population (millions, 1959)	Percentage of Main Nationality	Family of Principal National Language	Capital
Russian Soviet Federative Socialist Republic	1922	6,524,000	117.5	83.2	Slav	Moscow
Group A						
Ukraine S.S.R.	1922	232,000	41.9	88.1	Slav	Kiev
Byelorussia (White) S.S.R.	1922	80,100	8.1	80.0	Slav	Minsk
Moldavia S.S.R.	1940	13,100	2.9	65.4	Romance	Kishinev
Group B						
Estonia S.S.R.	1940	17,400	1.2	2.9	Finnic	Tallin
Latvia S.S.R.	1940	24,700	2.1	62.0	Baltic	Riga
Lithuania S.S.R.	1940	2,100	2.7	79.3	Baltic	Vilnyus
Group C						
Armenia S.S.R.	1936	11,600	1.8	88.0	Caucasian	Yerivan
Azerbaidzhan S.S.R.	1936	33,800	3.7	67.1	Turkic	Baku
Georgia S.S.R.	1936	27,800	4.0	63.3	Caucasian	Tbilisi (Tiflis)
Group D						
Kazakhstan S.S.R.	1936	1,063,000	9.3	29.6	Turkic	Alma Ata
Kirghiz S.S.R.	1936	76,400	2.1	40.5	Turkic	Frunze
Tadzhik S.S.R.	1929	54,800	2.0	53.1	Iranian	Dushanbe*
Turkmen S.S.R.	1925	188,400	1.5	60.9	Turkic	Ashkhabad
Uzbek S.S.R.	1925	154,000	8.1	62.0	Turkic	Tashkent
United Soviet Socialist Republic		8,593,000	208.826‡			Moscow

Note: The R.S.F.S.R. lies in Europe and Asia; Groups A and B lie in Europe; Group C in South Caucasus, and Group D in Middle Asia.

---
* Formerly Stalinabad.
‡ 1959 census total.

61

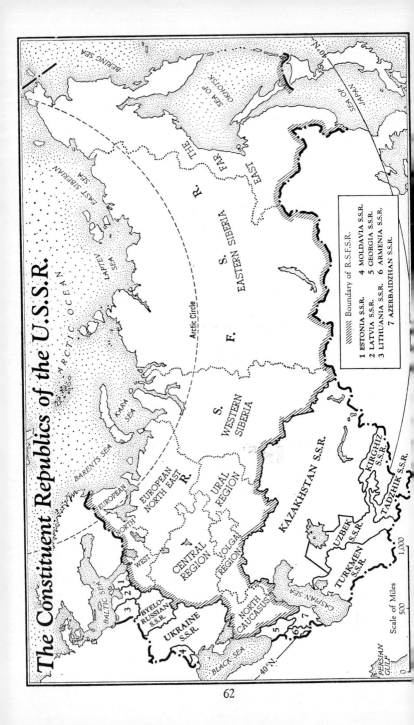

The Constituent Republics of the U.S.S.R.

BERING SEA

SEA OF OKHOTSK

SEA OF JAPAN

THE FAR EAST

EAST SIBERIAN SEA

LAPTEV SEA

ARCTIC OCEAN

Arctic Circle

R. S. F. S. R.

EASTERN SIBERIA

WESTERN SIBERIA

KARA SEA

BARENTS SEA

EUROPEAN NORTH EAST

URAL REGION

EUROPEAN NORTH

CENTRAL REGION

VOLGA REGION

KAZAKHSTAN S.S.R.

KIRGHIZ S.S.R.

TADZHIK S.S.R.

UZBEK S.S.R.

TURKMEN S.S.R.

BALTIC SEA

BYELO-RUSSIAN S.S.R.

UKRAINE S.S.R.

NORTH CAUCASUS

CASPIAN SEA

BLACK SEA

40° N.

PERSIAN GULF

//// Boundary of R.S.F.S.R.

1 ESTONIA S.S.R.   4 MOLDAVIA S.S.R.
2 LATVIA S.S.R.   5 GEORGIA S.S.R.
3 LITHUANIA S.S.R.   6 ARMENIA S.S.R.
                      7 AZERBAIDZHAN S.S.R.

Scale of Miles
0   500   1,000

62

Sixteen lie within the R.S.F.S.R., many being located in both the Volga-Ural and Caucasus regions. Occupying about one-fifth of the Union's territory, the A.S.S.R.'s range widely in area from the enormity of the Yakut to the relative smallness of the North Ossetian (see Table 4). They account, however, for only one-twelfth of the Union's population but include the relatively well-populated and industrial republics of the Moslem Bashkirs and Tatars. The national autonomy principle lies also behind the administrative units of the smaller minorities known as autonomous *oblasts* (regions) and national *okrugs* (areas); all of the latter and most of the former lie in the R.S.F.S.R.

The Soviet political structure has shown some flexibility: several A.S.S.R.'s, notably the Kazakh, Kirghiz, Moldavian, and Karelo-Finnish, were able to advance to Union status, although the last-named has now lost it. Similarly, an autonomous oblast may be upgraded to A.S.S.R. status, as in the case of the Tuvan A.O. in 1961. Temporary or permanent loss of status has also occurred where the Soviet rulers suspected lack of co-operation with the regime: thus the Crimean A.S.S.R. has disappeared to become a mere oblast of the Ukraine S.S.R. But despite such changes and minor adjustments of boundaries, the national units show a high degree of permanence, and it might appear that the U.S.S.R. has achieved some success in enlisting the co-operation of the nationalities.

For purposes of administrative convenience and efficiency the larger Union republics are also divided into oblasts, of which there are about 120. These areas, of greatly varying size in relation to population density, show more frequent changes than do the superior national-territorial units, since their number increases with ever-continuing and often rapid changes in the economy and regrouping of the population. The R.S.F.S.R., which contains more than 50 oblasts, has also six *krays* (territories). Some are of enormous extent, such as the Krasnoyarsk and Khabarovsk krays; they are so designated because they contain an autonomous oblast; their status however is merely that of the oblast. Like the oblasts, in responding to economic development, are those urban settlements which, starting

Table 4 *The Autonomous Soviet Socialist Republics of the U.S.S.R.*

Name	Area (sq. mi.)	Location	Attached to:	Population (millions, 1959)	Capital
Abkhaz	3,400	S. Caucasus	Georgia S.S.R.	0.40	Sukhumi
Adzhar	1,130	S. Caucasus	Georgia S.S.R.	0.24	Batumi
Bashkir	55,000	S. of Urals	R.S.F.S.R.	3.34	Ufa
Buryat	135,700	Transbaikal	R.S.F.S.R.	0.67	Ulan Ude
Chechen-Ingush	12,700	N. Caucasus	R.S.F.S.R.	0.71	Grozny
Chuvash	7,100	Volga-Urals	R.S.F.S.R.	1.10	Cheboksary
Dagestan	14,800	N. Caucasus	R.S.F.S.R.	1.06	Makhachkala
Kabardo-Balkarsk	3,800	N. Caucasus	R.S.F.S.R.	0.42	Nalchik
Kalmyk		Lower Volga	R.S.F.S.R.	0.18	Stepnoi
Karelian	68,900	N. European U.S.S.R.	R.S.F.S.R.	0.65	Petrozavodsk
Komi	156,200	N. E. European U.S.S.R.	R.S.F.S.R.	0.80	Syktyvkar
Mari	8,900	Volga-Urals	R.S.F.S.R.	0.65	Yoshkar Ola
Mordvinian	10,100	Volga-Urals	R.S.F.S.R.	1.00	Saransk
Nakhichevan		S. Caucasus	Azerbaidzhan S.S.R.	0.14	Nakhichevan
North Ossetian	2,600	N. Caucasus	R.S.F.S.R.	0.45	Ordzhonikidze
Tatar	26,100	Volga-Urals	R.S.F.S.R.	2.85	Kazan
Tuva	64,000	Upper Yenisei	R.S.F.S.R.	0.17	Kyzyl
Udmurt	16,200	Volga-Urals	R.S.F.S.R.	1.33	Izhevsk
Yakut	1,182,300	E. Siberia	R.S.F.S.R.	0.49	Yakutsk

as workers' settlements around industrial and mining sites, may grow sufficiently to be accorded city status.

THE GOVERNMENT OF THE U.S.S.R.

The political institutions of the Soviet Union include as its highest legislative body the Supreme Soviet, which is bicameral: (1) The Soviet of Nationalities reflects the Union's federal structure, since it is made up of 25 members from each Union republic, 15 from each autonomous republic, 5 from each autonomous oblast, and one from each national area. (2) The Soviet of the Union is elected by adult male and female suffrage on the basis of one member for every 300,000 inhabitants. The Union republics have a single elected chamber and have also their Council of People's Commissars. Soviets composed of "toilers' deputies" meet at every level—in the villages, rayons, oblasts, towns and cities—to discuss local affairs. Yet Soviet democracy, developed in a country where local and national self-government had only shallow roots, has its own peculiar character. For alongside, and supervising the formally elected institutions, is the well-organized Communist Party which holds securely and wields the powers of the state, in Moscow and throughout the Union. Khrushchev, like Stalin before him, as Secretary of the party's Central Committee, is the leader of the Presidium, formerly known as the Politburo. It is this small cabinet of party leaders that rules the Soviet Empire, which succeeded to that of the tsars.

5   *The Soviet Industrial Potential*

SOVIET propaganda and Soviet achievements in the economic field have obscured the remarkable industrial advance made by imperial Russia during the 50 years or so before World War I. While even at that time extensive manufacturing was derived from village handicrafts, great industrial progress had been made by using the power of the state and by introducing foreign experts and technologists. In both respects, government policy between 1860 and 1914, when Russia showed a high rate of industrial growth, recalls that of Peter the Great. He had said, "We need Europe for a few decades; then we can turn our backs on her," [1] and during the last half century of tsardom, as indeed in the Soviet decades which followed, Russia was at pains to make good its own deficiencies by drawing upon the higher knowledge and experience of western industrialists. Similarly, it derived from western countries, and especially from France, Great Britain, and Germany, a large part of the capital necessary for new industrial developments: one-half of that invested by 1900 had been obtained abroad.

The period 1860-1914 also witnessed the building of an effective railway system, above all in European Russia, but also one which linked this heartland to outlying territories in Asia beyond the Caucasus, the Caspian, and the Urals. In 1913 three million workers were employed in mining and manufacturing, and Russia's production of the basic requirements of modern industry was substantial: it then produced 29 million tons of coal, 9.2 million tons of oil mainly from Baku (the largest world producer), and 4.2 million

---

[1] B. H. Sumner, *Peter the Great and the Emergence of Russia* (London: English Universities Press Ltd., 1950), p. 203.

tons of steel. Since the 1870's the exploitation of coal in the Donetz basin and of iron ore in the Krivoi Rog deposit had succeeded to the point that the south had become Russia's major base for coal, ferrous metallurgy, and associated engineering industries.

Yet it remains true that, despite its great progress, the Russia of 1914 was an industrially backward country, noted more for its large exports of primary products—grain, timber, flax, and hemp—than for its industrial stature. The Industrial Revolution, which originated in Britain and pointed the way to production in scale by the use of steam-powered machines in factories, was slow to make its impact on Russia. This country long lived as a world apart, its social system in particular being uneasily adaptable to the requirements of modern industry. Industry, largely state-directed, had in earlier days depended on bondsmen—or serfs. And the survival into the twentieth century of a poor, illiterate, and only partially free peasantry and a small, landed intelligentsia of wealth precluded the emergence of both a strong middle class and a large domestic market. Nevertheless, given its vast extent, the territory of the empire contained an enormous potential for industry, little though this had been discovered or assessed. Likewise the large and rapidly increasing population of Russia promised the needed resources of labor and management, as well as a large and growing market. Thus, although in their early years of power the Bolshevik leaders were confronted with a disorganized country and an economy which was collapsing under excessive strains, the real resources of Russia were intact and available for exploitation. Moreover, Lenin, in particular, had given much thought to the problems involved and had devised policies which could be applied wherever conditions made this feasible.

During the years 1918-1921 of "war communism," the U.S.S.R. nationalized the land, the banks, large-scale industries, and trade. In and after 1921, however, the sheer necessities of survival involved a change of tactics and a temporary abandonment of socialist principles. Under the New Economic Policy private trade, the granting of foreign concessions, and the use of foreign bourgeois experts were all permitted. Also, the peasants were left with a considerable independence of state control. But by the end of the 1920's, all-Union control of the economy was being firmly established under the direction of the Communist leaders in Moscow. Control of agriculture and thus of food was being achieved in 1929 by the elimination of the wealthier *kulaks* (peasants) and by the collectivization of the peasant masses which began in 1930. On the industrial front the new shift towards a socialized direction was symbolized by the launching of the first Five-Year Plan, which started in 1928, and was reputedly fulfilled ahead of time in 1932.

THE SOVIET INDUSTRIAL EFFORT

The novelty of the Soviet industrial system resides in the state's assuming complete control and direction of industrial enterprise ostensibly on behalf of the sovereign proletariat. Private enterprise for personal profit was eliminated because it is considered the hallmark of allegedly capitalist exploitation of the worker. Only co-operative bodies approved by the state and under its effective supervision are allowed. The whole system is in no sense democratically controlled for, although councils at many levels offer the chance of discussion, policy decisions and directions are determined by the party leaders in Moscow and are issued as commands to be obeyed. A huge statistical machinery was devised, and also a State Planning Commission (Gosplan), the main responsibility of which was to elaborate long-term plans applicable to the whole country. These plans set goals for the different branches of the economy and express above all the government's intention continually to expand production in order to strengthen the state as an impregnable fortress for communism. The objectives included, in the first Five-Year Plan as in the current (1959-1965) plan, the overtaking and outstripping of the capitalist nations. They included, too, the raising of the living standards of the Soviet peoples to the levels enjoyed in the West.

However, the Soviet system of planning, which has never yet been other than one of state capitalism, strictly determines the priorities to be adopted. This has always meant that the major share of the country's resources of labor, management, and capital has been applied to the production of capital goods and that consumer consumption has been kept low, with the effect that enforced self-denial made possible a higher rate of output of mechanical energy, armaments, metals, machinery, and equipment. In part, this policy was rooted in the belief that the U.S.S.R.'s survival in an unfriendly world depended upon the sinews of war which derive from heavy industry. There was the continual fear of both an economic blockade and of attack by external enemies; the latter fear was well founded, as Hitler proved, and as the Allied intervention of 1918-1921 had foreshadowed.

While the plans are all-embracing, they are in no sense inflexible since they undergo continual adjustment in the course of the plan period. Their execution devolves on regional management councils and ultimately on the directors of individual plants. Members of the Communist Party, "the most exclusive disciplined political organization on earth,"[2] play an essential part by constant supervision, exhortation, and intervention. Criticism, the exposure of shortcomings, and dismissals are the penalties for failure and, if necessary, scapegoats are found. Clearly the task of planning and co-ordinating the U.S.S.R.'s economy to achieve maximum growth rapidly has been formidable. Advances have been by fits and spurts but always —even during World War II—striking. Success in priority sectors has been at times achieved only by the diversion of capital and effort from low priority sectors, such as those which are concerned with consumer goods. Clearly, too, the Soviet government, at least before 1939, had to depend reluctantly on substantial technological help and the importation of machines and equipment from the United States and western Europe. Yet the U.S.S.R. has unrelentingly pursued with speed and success its main objectives: to strengthen the state by industrialization, to make it as economically self-sufficient as possible, and to increase the material welfare of its

[2] H. R. Knickerbocker, *The Soviet Five-Year Plan and Its Effect on World Trade* (London: John Lane Bodley Head Ltd., 1931), p. IX.

citizens. Although much has been achieved, since it was late to start and enormous material resources are available, the U.S.S.R.'s industrial development has still a long way to go.

The growth of industrial production. Soviet industrial planning, with all its rigors and imperfections, has fast achieved a great expansion of production. By 1928, the 1913 level was exceeded; by 1940, a level six and one-half times that of 1928 had been achieved. Despite the German occupation between June 1941 and late in 1942 of the U.S.S.R.'s territory west of a line from Leningrad to Moscow and Stalingrad, by the end of World War II Soviet wartime industries were reaching an output little below that of 1940. Thereafter, despite the efforts required to rehabilitate war-devastated areas, a high rate of industrial progress has continued under successive plans. In late 1949, production reached 50 per cent above that of 1940, and in 1950 it was 75 per cent above that datum. In mid-November of 1958 Mr. Khrushchev claimed that industrial output had increased fourfold since 1940.

More recently Soviet planners have harped on a competitive note. Whereas in 1950 the U.S.S.R. produced less than 30 per cent of the volume of the United States' industrial production, in 1961 it was producing about 60 per cent of America's volume. At the end of the current Seven-Year Plan, i.e., in 1965, the U.S.S.R. expects to reach the United States' production level; by 1970 or 1980 it expects to exceed this level of production per head—no easy ambition. The scale of Soviet capitalization of the economy has grown staggeringly. The total investment in 1961 amounted to over one-quarter of the national income and was very nearly equal (at comparative prices) to that of the whole period of 1928-1940.[3] Global industrial output in 1961 rose by 9.2 per cent above that of 1960, exceeding the planned figure of 8.8 per cent, even though the working hours were reduced; there were as usual shortcomings in certain items, notably building materials. Factors which make for successful growth are the in-

[3] "The European Economy in 1961," Part I in *United Nations Economic Survey of Europe, 1961* (Geneva: 1962), Chap. II, p. 20.

creasing use of automative processes, standardization, full employ-ment, the annual increase of the labor force by 1.9 per cent in the fifties and by 1.7 per cent (as officially forecast) for the period 1960-1980, and the piece-rate system applied to wages which are more highly differential than in western countries. It should not be thought, therefore, that the high hopes set for the decade ahead will not be approached even if full success will await later growth.

A 20-year plan has been formulated for the years 1960-1980 which aims to secure for the Soviet peoples the highest standard of living and culture in the world.[4] By such time, according to Soviet theory, the state should be withering away on the threshold of the Com-munist paradise on earth. Not without reason did the American foreign correspondent Knickerbocker, writing in 1931, foresee that the U.S.S.R. would become a strong trade competitor with the West in the markets of the world.

Table 5 indicates the U.S.S.R.'s growth since 1913 in production of fuel, power, steel, cement, and some selected consumer industries, as well as the grandiose plans for future expansion.

The generalized figures given in Table 5 show that Soviet indus-trial output has always increased much more in heavy than in light industry. In the earlier plans, much attention was paid to the necessary infrastructure upon the basis of which heavy industries—making machine tools, machinery, equipment, and armaments—could be built. Therefore, electrification of the whole country was planned as early as 1920. Prospecting to discover the range and location of mineral resources, and mining developments, were given high priority (for example, gold and manganese ore were highly prized for their value as foreign exchange). Similar attention was given to the improvement of transport facilities—to the railways above all, but also to the waterways. Building materials had to be produced in ever-increasing abundance to keep pace with the

[4] *Ibid.,* pp. 49-58. National income is planned to quintuple between 1960 and 1980 and consumption per head to increase three and one-half to four times.

Table 5   *Industrial Production of the U.S.S.R. (Selected Items) 1913-1980*

	(1913)	(1940)	(1950)	(1961)	(1965 [plan*])	(1980 [plan])
Gross production of all industry (thousand million roubles at 1926-1927 prices)	16.2	138.5	240.0	—	—	—
Coal and lignite (million metric tons)	29.1	166.0	261.0	510	606	1,190
Petroleum (million metric tons)	9.2	31.0	38.0	166	240	700
Natural gas (000 million cubic meters)	—	—	6.2	60.9	150	700
Iron ore (million metric tons)	9.2	29.9	39.7	118	155	—
Steel (million metric tons)	4.2	18.3	27.3	70.7	96	250†
Electric power (thousand million kwh)	1.9	48.3	90.3	327	510	2,850
Cement (million metric tons)	1.8	5.7	10.2	50.9	84	234
Woolen textiles (million linear meters)	95.0	120.0	167.0	448	500 }	21,000
Cotton textiles (million square meters)	2270	3886	3815	4820	7850 }	
Artificial and synthetic fibers (metric 000 tons)	—	—	—	250	650†	—
Leather footwear (million pairs)	—	211.0	203.0	440	515	950

Source: "The European Economy in 1961," Part I in United Nations Economic Survey of Europe 1961 (Geneva: 1962), Ch. II, p. 52.
* The U.S.S.R.'s industrial output as a whole is planned to increase by 80 per cent between 1958 and 1965.
† Capacity.

programs for new factories, mines, power dams, and housing. (Expectably enough, the increasing output of cement [see Table 5] provides an interesting index of industrial growth.)

No less fundamental as part of the infrastructure of heavy industry was the creation of a skilled and semiskilled labor force, male and female, mainly from peasant material. In this area the educational effort has been sustained with an emphasis on higher education on its scientific and technical aspects. In addition, the problem of industrial location, on the basis of Lenin's ideas, was looked at afresh so that a less unbalanced geographical distribution of industry could be achieved and the strain on the overworked railway system could be in some measure relieved.

The resources of fuel and power. The Soviet estate is of sub-continental scale, and its natural resources are correspondingly great, becoming ever more abundant as prospecting proceeds. The U.S.S.R. has the greatest reserves of coal in the world and the highest annual production—about 520 million tons, made up of 400 million tons of mined hard coal and 120 million tons of brown coal, obtained mainly by open-pit extraction. Despite its increasingly abundant supplies of petroleum and natural gas, it has decided to more than double coal production by 1980 by the rapid exploitation of the brown coal reserves of Western Siberia, which will be chiefly utilized to generate electric power. The Donbas, with only 2.8 per cent of the country's geological reserves, still produces more than half of Soviet coking coal and about 35 per cent of total production. Its relative importance has fallen as output has grown from newer fields, notably those in Kuzbas (Western Siberia), Karaganda (Kazakhstan), Kizel and Chelyabinsk (Urals), Vorkuta (Pechora basin), and such Asiatic fields as Angren (Uzbek), Cheremkhovo (Central Siberia), and the Bureya basin and Sakhalin in the Far East. Due to its location, the brown-coal basin south of Moscow has long provided fuel especially for power stations; it is no longer scheduled to raise its production, chiefly because it is expensive to mine and because piped natural gas offers increasing supplies of cheaper fuel.[5] Indeed, natural gas, above all from the Volga-Ural area, Ukraine, and Azerbaidzhan, is now available in many large cities and will become ever more widely and cheaply available (see Table 5).

Russia was the first major exploiter of petroleum from the Caucasian fields, notably Baku. However, its principal source is now the Volga-Ural area, where the extensive Second Baku field more

[5] Natural gas accounted for 7.9 per cent of Soviet fuel consumption in 1960, but its share is expected to rise to 31 per cent in 1980.

than merits its name since it produced in 1961 no less than 70 per cent of the U.S.S.R.'s mounting output—more than enough for current domestic needs. The bulk of Soviet coal reserves lie in Siberia—some as yet untouched beneath the permanently frozen subsoil. However, the vast region beyond the Urals is largely dependent on piped or railed supplies of oil, although several relatively small local sources are available, and new strikes, such as the one of commercial scale recently found in northern Tyumen (Western Siberia), have been confidently forecast. Wood and peat also occur widely and serve many local needs.

Water power is being steadily exploited as great dams (in some cases, forming lakes of enormous size) are built on the major rivers: the Dnieper, Volga, Kama, Ob, Yenisei, Angara, Amur, and Sanga (in Armenia S.S.R.) among others. The greatest reserves of water power naturally lie in the mountainous regions of Central Asia, South Caucasus, and Eastern Siberia, although the Volga, with its many existing stations, including those at Rybinsk, Kuibyshev, and Volgograd, is a river of the Great Russian lowlands. In the field of power generation, the U.S.S.R. continues to build plants ever greater in scale and envisages long-term diversions of rivers to this end (for example, turning north-flowing rivers into the Volga). The Volgograd plant, which began operations in 1961, is the largest in the world, with a capacity of 2.5 million kw. The one at Bratsk on the Angara River, the first units of which are working, will eventually reach a capacity of 4.5 million kw.[6] Similarly, the new thermal plant on the Dnieper—Pridneprovskoye—achieves 1.2 million kw capacity and claims to be the largest of its kind in Europe. Beyond a doubt, when existing plans are realized, hydroelectricity will stake a somewhat larger claim as a source of industrial energy and will foster, in particular, electrochemical industries greedy for power. Yet, in 1960 this energy contributed only 22 per cent of the country's electricity output—292 thousand million kwh, six times that of 1940. By 1965

---

[6] "The European Economy in 1961," Part I in *United Nations Economic Survey of Europe, 1961* (Geneva: 1962), Chap. II, p. 20.

an integrated power grid will link up power stations in European U.S.S.R., South Caucasus, and Middle Asia; by 1980 Siberia will be included in a vast all-Union grid. Atomic power, which is already efficiently used by the icebreaker *Lenin,* should account for only 5 per cent of 1965 electricity output, since its production cost is not yet competitive.

Metallic and nonmetallic minerals. The U.S.S.R.'s known reserves of the many metallic and nonmetallic minerals necessary for modern industry are very large, although by no means fully prospected. Indeed, the search continues for new sources which are economically well located. Among the largest iron ore reserves are those at Krivoi Rog and Kerch (Ukraine), Magnitogorsk (Urals), and the Kursk magnetic anomaly, to which are added deposits in Kazakhstan, Siberia, and the Far East. The U.S.S.R. is the world's chief producer of manganese, above all from Chiatura (Georgia) and Nikopol (Ukraine). The Urals and Kazakhstan, in particular, hold large stores of nonferrous metals—copper, chrome, nickel, lead, silver, and zinc—while the Ukraine and Central Asia yield mercury. Tin, mainly from northeast Siberia (the Kolyma basin) and from Transbaikalia, probably is no longer a Soviet deficiency. Bauxite and nepheline for refining into aluminum occur widely from the Urals, Kazakhstan, and Eastern Siberia to the Far East. Ferroalloys, needed for special steels, are found in the mountain regions of North Caucasus, Central Asia, and the Far East. The U.S.S.R. has also its own Central Asian sources of uranium and thorium, such as those found in the eastern Pamir.

Agricultural raw materials. Soviet agriculture yields a wide range of products for light industry (see also Chapter 6). Among these products are potatoes (a source of alcohol for industry and for vodka), flax, hemp, silk and cotton fibers, sugar beet, grapes, and a range of oilseeds and grain. Also the U.S.S.R.'s pastoral farming provides supplies, not yet sufficient, for the processing of wool, hides, and meat. The extractive industries of the forests and seas supply respectively many timber-using industries and canneries.

THE CHANGING GEOGRAPHICAL DISTRIBUTION
OF SOVIET INDUSTRY

Large-scale industry, as distinct from handicrafts, was very narrowly located in the Russian Empire. Half of the industrial output came from the historic Russian region of the northwest and the center, which included the outstanding industrial concentrations at Moscow and St. Petersburg; another quarter from the South, mainly from the Ukraine; barely 10 per cent from the Volga cities and the Urals; and of the remainder, only very small shares derived from the South Caucasus and the vast dependencies beyond the Urals. More than half of Russia's coal, iron, and steel came from the Donbas in the south, and the rest from the Central Region and the Urals. The cotton textile industry was highly localized in the Central Region in and around the towns of Moscow and Ivanovo, remote from the principal sources of cotton. In short, Russia's modern industry was market-oriented, except where facts of economic geology were determinative (exemplified by the coal and iron-ore workings in the south, manganese working in Georgia, copper mining in Armenia, and oil drilling in Baku and North Caucasus).

Soviet plans have consistently sought not only to expand the economy where enterprises already existed but also rationally to extend it wherever feasible throughout the whole Union. It became increasingly clear that great untapped resources of soil, metals, fuel, and power awaited exploitation in the Urals and its enormous hinterland to the east—areas which are collectively known as the U.S.S.R.'s "Eastern Regions." Great efforts certainly have been made to increase the population of these vast spaces, and much capital, labor, and skilled direction have been applied to initiate and develop their industries. The accomplishment of this task was clearly sound policy for several reasons: (1) The new economic resources would contribute substantially to the strength of the economy. (2) It was strategically wise to redistribute an economy which left too much too vulnerable in European U.S.S.R. and too little (virtually nothing) in the Far East where the growing power of Japan threatened. (3) Given the vast scale of the U.S.S.R.'s territory, interregional trade imposed excessive strains on a hard-worked railroad system in moving such bulk goods as coal, oil, steel, machines, textile fibers, and grain over thousands of miles from European sources of supply. Accordingly, the policy was to create a series of regional bases of heavy industry in these rear areas, as also in South Caucasus, and to make them as far as possible economically self-sufficient.

The Eastern Regions account for 78 per cent of the Union's territory and consist of the following major units: the Urals, Western Siberia, Eastern Siberia, the Far East, and Middle Asia, which is made up of the Kazakhstan S.S.R. and the four Central Asian republics of Uzbek, Turkmen, Kirghiz, and Tadzhik. Table 6 shows the present areas of the components of the Eastern Regions and how their populations have grown during the last generation.

Table 6 *The Eastern Regions: Areas and Population Growth (1926-1959)*

	Area	Census Population (millions)		
	(000 sq. mi.)	(1926)	(1939)	(1959)
Urals	293	11.0	12.5	16.5
Western Siberia	936⎫	9.5	8.9	12.3
Eastern Siberia	2,782⎭		5.3	7.0
Far East	1,130	1.9	2.3	4.3
Kazakhstan S.S.R.	1,063	6.5	6.1	9.3
Central Asia	473	7.3	10.5	13.7
Totals (Eastern Regions)	6,677	36.2	45.6	63.1
Totals (U.S.S.R.)	8,600	147.0	170.5	208.8

The high rate of population and urban growth in the Eastern Regions, in response to Soviet policy, which included the resettlement there of workers evacuated from west European U.S.S.R. during World War II, is one mark of their industrial progress. The fact that less than one-third of the Union's population settled on more than three-quarters of its territory suggests that a labor shortage is felt there and that, in relation to their intrinsic resources, the Eastern Regions are still at an early stage of their economic development. The U.S.S.R. has consistently favored these areas in its capital investment allocations. Pre-World War II plans were successful to the extent that in 1940, the year before Hitler launched his assault, the Union was drawing from the Eastern Regions 59 million tons of coal and 6 million tons of steel. The operations of the Ural-Kuznetsk combine, based on the high-grade iron ores of Magnitogorsk and the coking coals of Kuzbas, had fostered the growth of two regions of heavy industry in the rear areas—in the Urals and Kuzbas, whose chief centers were respectively Sverdlovsk and Stalinsk (now Novokuznetsk). Of the two, the Urals were much the larger producer, not only of iron and steel, but also of armaments, machine tools, and heavy equipment; Kuzbas produced steel as well as coal. Other smaller centers of heavy industry had been started at Petrovsk, beyond Lake Baikal, at Komsomolsk in the Far East, and at Angren in Uzbek. Further, Karaganda in Kazakhstan was yielding coal, including coking coal, and offering supplies nearer to the Ural smelters than those of Kuzbas.

World War II greatly stimulated the industrial development of the Eastern Regions: 1300 large plants were evacuated from the west European U.S.S.R. ahead of the German military occupation and re-established there in accordance with prearranged plans. The industrial output of the Eastern Regions was officially reported to have doubled during the U.S.S.R.'s war years (mid-1941 to mid-1945) when they became a powerful supply base for ammunition, weapons, tanks, and aircraft for the Red Army. Indeed, Soviet prevision contributed vitally to the defense of the Union in its extreme peril.

The current 1959-1965 plan allocates 40 per cent of the Union's investment capital to the Eastern Regions where lie the greater part of its reserves of thermal and hydroelectric energy. Already by 1958 these areas provided 35 per cent of the U.S.S.R.'s electricity capacity; by 1965, their share is to rise to 46 per cent; it will rise yet higher when, during the 20-year plan period (1960-1980), their mighty rivers are harnessed, by stages, for the generation of electricity. Energy-intensive industries will increasingly figure in the economic development of Siberia and Kazakhstan, from which the Union will derive in 1965 71 per cent of its aluminum and 88 per cent of its copper supplies. Electric power, when it is ultimately made widely available by the construction of the grid system already contemplated, will prove especially convenient in the Eastern Regions, since their wide span of longitude necessarily effects a staggering of working hours. Piped petroleum and natural gas are already being brought into Western Siberia and Middle Asia and will be carried eastward to Krasnoyarsk and Irkutsk.

Meanwhile, the Eastern Regions depend to a considerable extent upon coal with its heavy demand on railroad transport; they contribute nearly half of the Union's coal output. Also they contribute nearly as much to steel supplies. Current and longer-term plans envisage several new centers of heavy industry related to local supplies of ore. One rising development is in south-central Siberia, and it is based on the coal of the Irkutsk-Cheremkhovo field, the water power of Bratsk and Irkutsk, and iron ore supplies of Novo Metelinsk. Other longer-term projects relate to the Tayshet region, and to those of Nerchinsk and Aldan farther east. In Kazakhstan the Temir-Tau ores and the Karaganda coal will support the iron and steel industry now being launched. The striking growth of the Eastern Regions' coal and steel output is shown in Table 7.

Table 7   *The Eastern Regions: Coal and Steel Production*
(million metric tons)

	(1913)	(1940)	(1950)	(1958)	(1965 [plan])
Coal, including lignite	3.4	58.9	123	230.5	303
Crude steel	0.9	5.9	13.3	23.7*	42

* 1957.

The majority of the 2,800 engineering plants envisaged under the 20-year plan will be located in the Eastern Regions where the chemical industry, which includes fertilizers, plastics, and synthetic rubber and fibers, will bulk increasingly large. Already some attempt has been made to locate modern textile mills nearer to the Central Asian supplies of cotton and silk.

6   *The Problem of Soviet Agriculture*

AGRICULTURE has always presented a major challenge to the Soviet leaders, for whom failure in this sector of the economy in earlier days might well have spelled disaster. Their philosophy was essentially an urban one, yet their country was at first predominantly agrarian. Although the Bolsheviks encouraged the poor peasants to partition the lands of the landlords and the richer peasants, they had no intention of allowing them a free hand that might jeopardize food supplies needed for the army and for workers in factories, mines, transport, and construction.

The peasants, though ignorant and illiterate, made up four-fifths of the proletariat and were astute enough where their own interests were concerned. How could they be induced to play their important part in a socialized economy so that a policy of all-out industrialization could succeed? How could the sharp differences of life in town and country be reduced? How also could the productivity of the Union's farmlands be raised from the existing low levels so as to strengthen the economy and to improve the living and working standards of the peasant? These were hard problems, and a solution was found only through force and at a cost of much suffering and mortality. The socialistic solution called for was found in collectivization—a revolutionary departure for which neither Marx nor Lenin had provided more than a few shadowy outlines.

THE REORGANIZATION OF FARMING

The campaign began in 1928 when the government liquidated some 750,000 Kulak families who were farming sizable holdings and were making too much profit by private enterprise. Then followed the invitation to peasant farmers to pool freely their land, livestock, and farm implements and thus to create collective farms which would be run on communal lines. Whereas Lenin had always insisted that the peasants be taught and led gently to accept necessary changes, his successor, Stalin, beset by many serious difficulties, pursued his policy of collectivization relentlessly—indeed, with the soullessness with which he charged party officials at this time.

The government's determination led to a head-on clash with the peasants. It was peasant resistance to official policy and their slaughter of draft animals (without which much land was left unsown), rather than bad weather, which accounted for the two successively poor harvests of 1931 and 1932 and the subsequent famine in the Ukraine, North Caucasus, Lower Volga, and even Western Siberia. Deaths due to the 1932-1933 famine alone have been variously estimated: two conservative estimates are two and three to four millions, respectively. Yet Stalin's will prevailed, and from 1933 collective farms became the norm throughout the Union. The system proved itself viable under the strains of World War II when tractors, manpower, and even horses were withdrawn for the use of the Red Army. And in postwar years, the system has been established in all the European satellite neighbors of the U.S.S.R. except Poland.

Despite the manner of its institution and the peasants' lack of enthusiasm, the collective-farms system has well served the needs and purposes of the Soviet leaders. Whereas the tsars had to deal with no less than 25 million peasant holdings, the U.S.S.R. had to deal with only 250,000 large, though regionally unequal, farms. By 1950, as a result of farm amalgamations, this number was reduced to 125,000, and by 1962 to only 45,000. Although the land was declared the property of the state, thus robbing the peasants of the visible profit of the revolution, the shares allotted to collective farms were legally inalienable and granted for their use in perpetuity. Further, the collective farms were a means by which the government could treat farming as an industry, include it in all-Union plans, and firmly direct and control its operations. In its efforts to increase agricultural productivity, reduce the manpower needed on the farms (thus freeing millions for work in the factories and the mines), and raise the peasants' standards of work and of living, the state set about providing tractors, trucks, combine harvesters, fertilizers, electricity, and scientific and technical advice. Real strides had been made in these directions before World War II.

However, the chief virtue of the collective-farms system for the government was that it could collect with relative ease necessary supplies of agricultural produce. The obligatory deliveries which these farms make to the state are calculated on a predetermined scale proportionately to the area of the farm and at prices fixed by the state. The state makes purchases, too, at its own prices. Until their abolition in 1958, the machine tractor stations were paid in kind for their services to the farms and the state bought these supplies. Since the obligatory deliveries are determined in advance as a percentage of the anticipated and not the actual yield, the farm, and not the state, is the sufferer if the harvest falls short of expectation. During the years 1933-1940, the state actually received nearly one-third of the grain crop. It was thus in a strong position for supplying the fast-growing towns and the armed forces, and also for maintaining a stockpile and for making exports. The farms could no longer hoard grain and so profit in times of scarcity; rather, the state held and controlled the stocks and could ration their use in times of shortage, such as occurred during 1929-1934 and 1941-1945. Another signal advantage to the state was that the large profits made from selling the processed agricultural goods enabled it to finance its policy of industrialization.

Under Stalin's regime, and even since, the peasants, renamed "collective farmers," constituted the hardest-worked and worst-paid class in the Soviet Union. Indeed, their work as agricultural proletarians under foremen, themselves directed by higher officials of the farm which was itself linked by a chain of command with Moscow, contributed vitally if indirectly to the successive advances on the industrial front. Yet the collective farm system offered some incentives and long-term prospects as it also offered the chance of social and cultural betterment in urbanized villages. The collective farm, made up of many peasant households, at least provides the facilities of a kindergarten, primary school, library, and community center. It requires a range of technical, administrative, and specialist staff. Wages depend on the productivity of the farm and, like those in industry, are based on piecework, and are highly differential in relation to the skill required. A certain minimum of work is required from members of the farm, nearly two-fifths of whom were women in 1937, and payment is mainly in kind—in grain. While these supplies serve primarily for subsistence, the farmer can dispose of any surplus in the free market. But he has fortunately another source of income, which is the produce of a private plot or garden that is in area from one-half to one and one-quarter acres. Since he is allowed to keep it for his own use, he can grow potatoes, vegetables, and fruit; breed a few livestock, including a cow and poultry; and keep bees. Moreover, since 1933 he has been permitted to sell any surplus produce on the free market, and nowadays he is willing to travel far in search of the best markets.

The retention of these private holdings, where to a modest degree the farmer can indulge his private initiative for private profit, involved a compromise of its socialist principles which the government could not avoid. Expectably enough, the farmer's interests and energies are divided as he works in turn both for his own profit and for that of the communal farm. In 1939 about four and one-half million acres of land in private plots was detached and turned over to communal use, and the ultimate elimination of the private plots is doubtlessly necessary to realize fully the Communist ideal.

State farms. Another system of farming was devised more closely along factory lines, where wages were paid in cash on a piecework basis and where no private plots were permitted. The so-called state farms, which are intended to raise agronomic standards by experiment and research, fall into several categories. Some are devoted to livestock breeding or to grain cultivation and seek to discover the best breeds and the best seeds for the particular region in which they operate. Some are concerned with suburban horticulture; others with special crops, such as cotton, tea, tobacco, fruit, and vineyard products; and yet others specialize in poultry raising. There were nearly 4,000 of these farms established in the different climatic regions of the Union in 1939, and the number increased to 7,000 by 1962. It was the state farms which carried out a large part of the plowing-up campaign in the virgin and fallow lands which was launched in 1953. And it was believed until recently that they represented the highest organizational form of socialist agriculture.

THE DRIVE TO RAISE AGRICULTURAL PRODUCTION

The land itself. In its efforts to raise the production of food, fodder, and raw materials, the Soviet government has had to wage a struggle, not only with the peasants, but also with the land—an even less amenable opponent, for which Soviet planned targets do not carry the force of law. The vast estate of the Union, even though it offers widely varied agricultural opportunities, imposes severe physical restrictions. Only 7 per cent of the surface was cultivated in 1913; this proportion rose to 9 per cent in 1955, and has reached 10 per cent today only after emergency efforts. Can this proportion be increased much and, if so, at what cost? Or must an alternative be sought in a more efficient organization of farming?

Commercial agriculture has at present virtually no possibilities in nine-tenths of the country. The U.S.S.R. occupies high latitudes: the latitude of Odessa (Black Sea) is the same as that of Duluth, Minnesota, and the U.S.S.R.'s nearest geographical analogue is Canada. Accordingly, much of its surface is under coniferous forest and too cold for crops. Some is even under tundra vegetation and parts, where it dips south in Middle Asia, is sheer desert. Permanently frozen subsoil, marshes, and mountains occupy large areas. Further, even where the land is relatively at its best for grain cultivation, the precipitation is near the margin and sharply variable from year to year. The U.S.S.R.'s so-called "dry areas"—astride the Volga and southern Urals, and in Western Siberia and Kazakhstan —accounted for 40 per cent of the area sown to grain in 1953 and for 50 per cent in 1958. In those areas precipitation averages between 11 and 16 inches a year, of which more than one-third falls during the growing season when up to six inches is lost through evaporation. These dry areas are drier, and hotter in summer, than the similar regions in Montana and southern Alberta. Necessarily, nature imposes here to make good yields only periodic and defies the ever-raised Soviet harvest targets.

These dry areas coincide with the easterly parts of the steppe which is broadest in the European south—in Moldavia, the Ukraine, and North Caucasus—and even these traditionally productive and better watered lands suffer periodically from short falls of rain. While the northern flank of the steppe zone, where wooded steppe vegetation (now cleared) was formerly prevalent, included the famous Black-earth soils that are rich in carbonate of lime, these occur to only about 25 million acres beyond the Urals in Western Siberia. Another climatic hazard of the steppe lands is the *sukhovey,* a dry and scorching southeast or east wind which can shrivel the crop before the harvest. In short, even though it has had specific successes in increasing the area of sown land and its productivity, the U.S.S.R. has not managed to eliminate harvest fluctuations; nor can it, under the existing agricultural system, which is inefficient judged by North American standards, add much to its yields except by heavy applications of capital, fertilizers, and technological and scientific energy. The drainage of such marshes as those of the Pripet River in Byelorussia and the irrigation of such dry lands as those in Central Asia and the Volga region are costly undertakings. Hitherto, agriculture has been the Cinderella of the Soviet economy; it will have to lose this status, if plans are not to miscarry.

Yet in the physical background to Soviet farming, many favorable features are evident. There are enormous stretches of natural grazing and meadows, although these are only seasonally available. The wide cleared expanses of the wooded and grass steppes present level or gently undulating surfaces for which modern mechanized farm techniques are excellently adapted. Central and northwesterly parts of European U.S.S.R. provide conditions well suited to the potato and vegetables which are grown in virtually all the farming regions of the Union. The range of climate, too, permits intertropical cultivation through irrigation, so that only a few basic crops—notably natural rubber, jute, coffee, and cocoa—fail to find an edaphic niche.

The increase in crop production. For sheer volume of production of grain, potatoes, and textile fibers, the U.S.S.R. stands very high indeed in the world table. The picture is marred somewhat by the fact that—unlike Canada, for example—it has so large a population to supply. Soviet statistics are sufficiently plentiful to show the increase in cultivated area and crop production, and also the far from impressive progress made in pastoral farming. In assessing the significance of these figures, several points should be borne in mind: (1) that the U.S.S.R.'s territory was smaller between 1917 and 1940 than in 1913, but became little less than that of 1913 after World War II; (2) that during that war nearly half of its cultivated areas was fought over and devastated; and (3) that its population has grown, if unevenly, during the period covered.

Bread occupies so high a position in the diet of Soviet citizens (even though, within recent years, higher wages in the towns have caused some change here, including a larger demand for meat) that attention should first be focused on the production of grain. Actually between 1928 and 1932, when agriculture was at a very low ebb, and 1954 and 1958, when the emergency plowing-up campaign was giving results, the area sown to grain increased by 28 per cent; but so did the population (see Table 8).

Table 8   *Expansion of the Grain Area and Increase of Population*

	(1928-1932)	(1933-1936)	(1937-1940)	(1940)	(1953)	(1956-1958)
Area under grain (million acres)	246	257	255	275	267	315
Estimated population (millions)	156	161	169	192*	190	200

* The increase in 1940 was due to the accession of territories. (See also Chapter 8.)

Any improvement in the grain situation—and it should be remembered that the 1928-1932 period witnessed rural disorganization and sporadic famines—can therefore be found only in improvements of yield which have in fact taken place. The average grain yield during 1954-1958 was 0.4 tons per acre, as compared with 0.3 tons per acre during 1928-1932. The production of technical crops, which provide both foodstuffs and raw materials, has been greatly increased, chiefly by expanding their cultivated areas. (In the case of flax, however, this expansion was achieved by higher yields from a reduced area.) By a virtual trebling of the irrigated area since 1913, the cotton crop, for example, has grown five or six times since tsarist days; the sugar-beet crop has more than trebled, although attempts to grow the beet in drier easterly areas have not proved very successful; and the area under sunflower, too, has been much enlarged. However, tea growing in Georgia, which yields over 100,000 tons of leaf tea, is largely a Soviet development. Table 9 shows how the production of technical crops has grown, how the grain position has improved since the last years of Stalin (1949-1953), and how ambitious are the goals set for 1965.

Livestock and animal produce. In this branch of farming the U.S.S.R. has been least successful, despite its large resources of graz-

Table 9 *The U.S.S.R. Agricultural Production of Principal Food Crops and Raw Materials**
(yearly averages, in million metric tons)

	(1909-1913)	(1949-1953)	(1954-1958)	(1959-1961)	[1965-(plan)]
Cereals	72.5	80.9	113.2	132.5	164-180
Potatoes	30.6	75.7	83.4	——	147
Sugar beet†	10.1	21.1	35.5	——	76-84
Sunflower seeds‡	1.0	2.51	3.86	3.9	5.5
Vegetables	5.5	10.0	14.0	——	——
Grapes	0.6	0.8	1.3	——	6.9
Raw cotton	0.68	2.51	3.86	4.47	5.7-6.1
Flax	0.3	0.2	0.4	——	0.6

* Within the areas now included in the Soviet Union.
† The proportion of sugar extracted varies between 10 and 15 per cent.
‡ These are an important supply of fats for human consumption.

ing lands and its practice of ley farming. No better indication of the peasants' attitude towards collectivization can be found than the fact that they preferred to slaughter their livestock rather than hand it over to communal use. Long after collectivization had been firmly established, total livestock numbers failed to reach those of 1928. Thereafter, losses due to World War II, especially through enemy occupation of west European U.S.S.R., inflicted another severe setback: the number of cattle (including cows) in 1957 still fell below that of 1928, as shown in Table 10. The recovery in more recent years falls far short of planned objectives.

Table 10 *Livestock Numbers*
(in million head)

	Total Cattle	Number of Cows	Pigs	Sheep and Goats*
1928	66.8	33.2	27.7	114.6
1938	50.9	22.7	25.7	96.6
1957	61.4	29.0	40.8	119.8
1961	81.9	36.3	66.4	144.1

* Goats made up less than 10 per cent of this category in recent years.

This stock is shared between collective and state farms and private peasant ownership. Before World War II, between two-thirds and three-quarters of the animals were owned by the peasants. This position is now largely reversed, for the percentage shares of livestock held by collective and state farms in 1961 are 71.1 in cattle, 55.4 in cows only, 74.1 in pigs, and 75.6 in sheep and goats.

It is evident that, given the U.S.S.R.'s virtually closed economy, supplies of meat, butter, and milk—as well as of wool, hides, and leather—have failed to increase fast enough to achieve the production targets set (see Table 11). By building up a strong fishing fleet, fitted with the latest equipment, and operating it especially in the open northern seas and in Pacific waters, the U.S.S.R. has succeeded in doubling its prewar catch.

Soviet grain yields. Major changes in the geographical distribution of the Soviet grain cultivation have been a deterrent to higher

Table 11 *Production of Livestock Products*
(million metric tons, except for eggs)

	(1913)	(1937-1940) average	(1953)	(1959-1961) average	(1965 [plan])
Meat and fat	5.0	3.4	5.8	8.8	16
Milk	29.4	28.9	36.5	62.0	100-105
Butter	——	——	——	0.845* (1959)	1.1
Granulated sugar	1.4	2.2 (1940)	——	8.4 (1961)	9.25-10.0
Eggs (000 million)	11.9	10.0	16.1	28.3	37.0
Fish (catch)	——	1.6†	——	3.1 (1959)	4.6
Wool‡	0.2	——	0.2	0.4 (1962)	0.5

* Includes farm and household production.
† 1936.
‡ State procurement.

yields. Although some success has been achieved in increasing grain cultivation in more northerly regions, such as in the central European U.S.S.R., there have been steady decreases in the grain area of the European south. The northern area wheat is almost entirely winter-sown, thus producing a higher yield. The enormous expansion in the grain area—from 1954 to 1956, 90 million acres of virgin and fallow land were brought under the plow—relates almost wholly to the dry areas: the northern Kazakhstan, Western Siberia, Volga, and Ural regions in that order. And these are regions where grain can be sown only in spring and, for this reason alone, they give lower yields. Over 70 per cent of the Union's wheat lands are now spring-sown, a complete reversal of the position before World War II.

While crop yields run low in the U.S.S.R., as is to be expected with extensive mechanized farming, both annual and regional variations are considerable. The 1965 plan, which seeks to raise output steeply, clearly hopes for greatly increased yields of both breadstuffs and fodder. But harvest fluctuations are marked, especially in regions on or near the rainfall margin—where most of the Union's grain lands lie. For the country in general, during the years 1953-1958, the highest grain harvest (in 1958) was 65 per cent above the lowest (in 1953). But the contrast was much sharper in the principal granary regions. During these years, the Ukraine's production ranged between 14.3 and 31.3 million tons; it achieved its highest in 1961. And Moldavia and North Caucasus showed a range of over 100 per cent. The situation is much the same or worse in the new granary of the Union. Harvest yields in the Volga Region ranged between 5.9 and 14.6 million tons; those of Kazakhstan between 10.6 million tons in 1956 and 22.0 million tons in 1958; and those of Western Siberia suffered similar fluctuations. It would appear that climate—or more precisely, drought—is the main determinant.

THE REGIONAL DISTRIBUTION
OF AGRICULTURAL PRODUCTION

The most productive grain lands are the steppes that extend east northeast from the Moldavia S.S.R. to northern Kazakhstan and to the outer limits of the Omsk and Altai regions of Western Siberia. The arable lands of the European south—in the Ukraine, Moldavia, and North Caucasus—account for one-third [1] of the U.S.S.R.'s grain harvest, over 75 per cent of its maize, and nearly 30 per cent of its wheat. Virtually all winter-sown, wheat has steadily replaced rye as the Union's principal bread crop since the 1930's. Traditionally, these lands—the Ukraine in particular—were the granary for the well-populated but grain-deficit lands of central and northern Russia. The population growth, however, has largely eliminated their surplus of wheat. It is the steppe lands of Kazakhstan and Western Siberia farther east, where grain must be sown after the snow has melted in late spring, which now take precedence as the chief source of surplus food grains. Together they have yielded 30 per cent of the Union's grain and over 42 per cent of its wheat, which really amounts to a monoculture in these newly developed lands. A third outstanding producer of grain is the Central Region of European U.S.S.R., if this is taken to include both the Moscow Industrial

[1] The percentages given in the text and tables of this section are based on the yearly average of production for the years 1956-1958 and the Soviet census of population for January 15, 1959.

Region and the Central Black-earth Region to the south of it. These together produced 20 per cent of the country's grain, including 12 per cent of its wheat, which was winter-sown. But because of its relatively high population density and high degree of urbanization, this region takes its place among the grain-deficit ones. Indeed, many of the major regions of the U.S.S.R. are unable to meet their own grain requirements.

The deficiency areas lie in the northern European and Asiatic U.S.S.R., where climate severely limits or precludes cultivation; South Caucasus, where the extent of mountains and aridity in the Azerbaidzhani lowlands greatly restricts the cultivated area; Central Asia, where irrigated crops, above all cotton, largely monopolize the small areas of cultivation; and the Far East, where food crops have never been able to catch up with the rapid population increases caused by immigration.

Tables 12 and 13, by setting together percentages of the Union's population and wheat harvest, show, on the one hand, the regions which offer a large surplus of wheat, and on the other, those which must supplement their own insufficient production.

Table 12   *Main Wheat-Surplus Regions*

	Percentage of the U.S.S.R.'s Population	Percentage of the U.S.S.R.'s Wheat Crop
Kazakhstan S.S.R.	4.5	24.0
Western Siberia	5.9	18.4

Table 13   *Main Wheat-Deficit Regions*
(in order of decreasing deficiency)

	Percentage of the U.S.S.R.'s Population	Percentage of the U.S.S.R.'s Wheat Crop
Northern European U.S.S.R.	5.5	0.2
Central Asia	7.6	1.2
Far East	2.1	0.6
South Caucasus	4.6	1.3
Central European U.S.S.R.	19.0	12.0

In contrast to these groups of regions are others which more or less achieve the goal of regional self-sufficiency in grain production. Two such regions are: the Ural industrial region which, with 7.9 per cent of the Union's population, averaged during 1956-1958 7.6 per cent of the Union's wheat harvest; and Eastern Siberia, where the comparable figures are respectively 3.4 and 4.4, which suggest that it enjoys a margin above its local needs. The surplus now available from the European south is small because, even though it produces 30 per cent of the Union's wheat, it now makes up 27 per cent of the population.

This analysis should emphasize how important are successful grain harvests in the European south and in Kazakhstan and Western Siberia if the Union is to meet requirements for human and animal consumption, the stockpile, and occasional calls from its satellite neighbors. It is no less evident that large interregional shipments of grain are still necessary to supplement the domestic production of the deficit regions. South Caucasus depends on supplies from North Caucasus and the Ukraine, where shipments may be made from Azov-Black seaports. The Central Asian Republics draw on the surplus of Western Siberia by way of the Turkestan-Siberian railway. The Soviet Far East, furthest removed from the surplus-producing lands, must import either by railroad from Western Siberia or, more economically (and long a common practice), from Vancouver across the Pacific.

The increased production of maize for fodder—and of sugar beet and sunflower seed for food—have been achieved largely by expanding their cultivated areas rather than by striking increases of yield per acre. The maize harvest was reported at 13.2 million tons for 1961, as compared with a yearly average of 7.8 million tons for 1956-1958. Sugar-beet production rose from 42.2 million tons in 1956-1958 to 57.7 million tons in 1960. The sunflower crops increased little during these years; the production of seed averaged nearly four million tons a year (1959-1961). In maize, sugar-beet, sunflower seed, and wheat returns, the Ukraine and adjacent areas of Moldavia and North Caucasus stand highest in yield per acre. However, in sugar-beet harvesting Kazakhstan and Kirghiz do better, for the good reason that it is an irrigated crop there. The lowest per-acre yields of these crops are obtained in the Ural, Volga, and West Siberian regions. Grain yields are low too in the north European U.S.S.R. and Central Asia. Potatoes and vegetables give their heaviest yields in the northwest of the European U.S.S.R., including the Baltic states and Byelorussia. In nongrain crops, other than vegetables, production is highly localized by conditions of climate. Flax and hemp are grown in the European R.S.F.S.R., Byelorussia, and the Ukraine. Over 80 per cent of the sugar-beet crop comes from the black-earth regions of the Ukraine and Central Region, which also produce most of the Union's tobacco. Sunflowers and vines have a wide distribution in the central and southern parts of European U.S.S.R. and grow also in South Caucasus and Central Asia. The cultivation of cotton, tea, and citrus fruits is very narrowly localized. Watered lands in Uzbek produce nearly two-thirds of the Union's cotton, although Tadzhik—praised for its high-staple cotton—Kazakhstan, Turkmen, and Azerbaidzhan also contribute. Tea and citrus fruits are grown on the wet Black Sea coastal slopes of Georgia.

PROSPECTS FOR SOVIET AGRICULTURE

Mr. Khrushchev's admissions and continual concern testify beyond doubt that all is far from well with Soviet farming and the Soviet countryside. Agriculture was stagnating at the time of Stalin's death (1953) and, although much has been done since—by plowing up on a grand scale, raising steeply the state's prices for produce, disbanding the machine tractor stations, and increasing production of fertilizers—agriculture remains the weakest sector of the economy and resists fulfillment of the Union's plans. As industrial output mounts and the urban population and standard of living rise, the demand grows for meat which the farms appear unable fully to meet.

One of the difficulties of over-all planning of a state's economy is that, since all parts of the economy are co-ordinated, the failure of any part detracts from the success of the whole. The long-term plans which look forward to 1970 and 1980 and to rent-free apartments and free local travel, gas, electricity, and social services for the sick and aged could clearly be stultified if the countryside failed to provide that "horn of plenty to which everyone will have access."

There is no crisis in Soviet agriculture in the sense that the U.S.S.R. need envisage any falling off of agricultural output such as would seriously threaten its social and economic well-being. Agricultural production is enormous, despite the disasters and destruction caused by World War I, civil war accompanied by intervention of the western Allies, and Hitler's invasion. It must be recognized too that for agricultural programs the Soviet Union is in no sense as well endowed by nature as the United States: the Union has only two acres of cultivated land per capita as compared with four acres in the United States. Yet, when all allowances are made, it must be noted that Soviet agriculture is inefficient by North American standards, partly a result of its socialized organization. To illustrate: whereas Soviet steel and machine tools can compete on equal terms in the world market, the cost of meat in the U.S.S.R., in terms of man hours, is four times, the cost of wheat double, that in the United States. On strictly economic ground, which Soviet ideology precludes, the U.S.S.R. would do well to buy part of its foodstuffs in the world market in return for industrial products. But ideology insists that a socialized agriculture is the only and best solution, yet it is applied to peasants whose mentality is essentially capitalist in that they understand and appreciate profit making and are less interested in so-called material incentives which materialize inadequately. The alleged crisis in Soviet agriculture which arose in the early months of 1962 and focused attention on the 1961 failures of the plans for meat, milk, and grain should be set against the high targets raised for 1971 and 1981, which can hardly be closely approached if the more modest plans for 1965 miscarry (see Table 14).

New measures now being put into practice indicate once again the assertion of state power without which the Soviet farm system functions unsatisfactorily. It appears that the abolition of the ma-

Table 14   *Certain Targets Set for 1971 and 1981*

	(1961)	(1971)	(1981)
Agricultural output	100	250	350
Meat output	100	300	390
Industrial output	100	250	600
Peasants' real income	100	210	410

chine tractor stations, which left the collective farms free to hold and use their own tractors and equipment, achieved little positive gain in harvest yields. Stalin's system of rotation farming, which was intended to improve the grasslands, is now denounced and to be abandoned, mainly because collective farmers pasture their own livestock on the communal grass. The state farms, formerly so vaunted, have also failed to give satisfaction. Accordingly, regional production directorates have been set up which, under direction from Moscow, will literally manage the farms, to the end that all-Union plans shall be fulfilled. But it would appear that much heavier investment in agriculture and much greater incentives are necessary to achieve success in this lagging branch of the economy.

7   *The Facilities for Transport*

FACILITIES of transport and communication are essential if a state is to carry out its functions in administration, economic life, and defense. Provision of these facilities is all the more necessary if the state is, like the Soviet Union, of great territorial scale and has a centralized form of government. Without sufficient means of transport, large areas may lie outside effective state control, as they do in many of the South American states. Russia had already demonstrated the serious disadvantages of inadequate transport by its defeat in the Crimean War of 1854-1856 and in the Russo-

Japanese War of 1901-1904. In the first case, without railways south from Moscow, Russia failed against its enemies France and Britain, whose distant bases were reached by sea. In the second, although she had just completed the single-track Trans-Siberian railway, Russia fought at great distances from its main base a maritime enemy that was operating from a base near to the theater of war.

The U.S.S.R. has always grasped the need for an effective system of transport as a prerequisite of Soviet leadership, economic planning, and political control. Accordingly, transport has been given its due share in capital investment. The main regions of the U.S.S.R. are integrated above all by the railroads, while aircraft links the capital with remote regions, devoid of railroads, as well as the major cities with each other. The rivers, which played an all-important part in earlier times, carry heavy freight but only in a small and decreasing share. Inland seas and lakes play a useful role, while coastwise transport has only limited opportunities since great distances and climatic difficulties are involved. Similarly, road haulage, though increasing, is very small in relative scale because few motor roads exist. Of rising importance today and in the years ahead are the pipelines for oil and the transmission lines for electricity.

Table 15   *Freight Transport by Different Means*
(in percentages)

	(1913)	(1940)	(1956)	(1960)	(1965) [plan]
All means (000 million ton/kms.)	11.5	487.4	1,301.0	1,600.0	2,500
Railroad	57.4	85.1	82.9	80	72.9
Sea	17.4	4.9	6.3	7 }	14.4
River	24.9	7.4	5.4	5* }	
Road	0.1	1.8	3.7	5	5.3
Pipeline	0.3	0.8	1.6	2*	7.4

* Slightly above this figure.

THE RAILROAD SYSTEM

During the last hundred years, Russia and the U.S.S.R., in turn, have depended for their viability on railroads which function the year round (just as the British Empire depended on ocean routes). In 1913 Russia had 43,000 miles of lines, three-quarters of which were in its populous and developed regions west of the Volga, and they provided the essential links with the major seaports and with the outlying provinces in South Caucasus, Central Asia, Siberia, and the Far East. Moscow, with an outer ring line around it, was and remains the hub of the whole system. The railroads are also well developed in the Donbas, yet even at its closest in European Russia, the railroad pattern is more open than that of western Europe. East of the Volga, Russia had only single-track lines, with short feeders to them and no real network. Vast areas beyond the Urals to the north and east had no railroads at all then, nor have they now, except for the short Norilsk-Dudinka line, even though the U.S.S.R.'s length of state railroads has reached 78,000 miles. Clearly, such wide, scantily settled, and undeveloped regions do not justify the high capital costs of railroad construction. To rely on other means of transport—aircraft, river ships and rafts, and even sleds drawn over the ubiquitous snow ways of winter—would be more sensible. Given their prime purpose of distributing goods between centers of production and of consumption, the railroads connect the settled and productive areas and stimulate development along their course. The lengthening of the system achieved during the Soviet period has included the doubling of many single-track lines, the construction of relief lines to ease the burden of those which are overworked, and the provision of wholly new lines required by planned economic developments, mostly in the eastern regions.

Within the reduced territory of the U.S.S.R., there were at the start only 36,590 miles of railway, but as early as 1920 a new line was built to connect Kazan with Sverdlovsk, industrial capital of the Urals. The Turkestan-Siberian railroad (Turksib), completed in 1931, was another early addition. Logically designed to link up two major regions of complementary production, it connects Western Siberia with its timber and grain supplies, and Central Asia with its cotton, wool, silk, fruit, and wine products. With the growth of industrial production under the early Five-Year Plans, the strain imposed on the railroads grew excessive. During 1928-1933, for example, the railroads increased by only 7 per cent in length but by 82 per cent in traffic.[1] In 1935 Kaganovich, a member of the Politbureau, was put in charge of railroad transport which was given top priority until 1937. Greater investment was made and over one-fifth of the country's iron and steel output was consumed by railroad development in 1935 alone. New lines were commissioned, such as a third trunk line between Moscow and Donbas, while multiple trackage, new equipment, and automatic breaking and signaling were installed. Electrification made its beginnings in the 1930's, the line from the port of Murmansk to Leningrad being among the first. The substitution of diesel for steam engines on the Trans-Caspian railway, which crosses waterless desert, was another improvement in efficiency.

Metallurgical developments in Kazakhstan account for the lines which joined the copper refinery at Kunrad on Lake Balkhash with the mines at Karsakpai to the west and with the newly exploited coal field at Karaganda to the north. Perhaps the most outstanding railway improvement before World War II was the doubling of the Trans-Siberian railway. In short, although more heavily worked than those of any other country, the Soviet railroads were reasonably well equipped to play their vital part during World War II. Removal to rear areas of locomotives and rolling stock from invaded territory was successfully effected. Railroad workers were, it is true, subjected to martial law in 1943 and to close control by party officials, but at least they were accorded the rations for manual workers at a level second only to those of the Red Army. To meet rising war needs, more railroads were built during that period, notably one linking the Pechora coal field to the Leningrad-Moscow trunk and another running from Saratov to Stalingrad along the right bank of the Volga.

Military operations during 1941-1943 inflicted severe destruction

[1] Harry Schwarz, *Russia's Soviet Economy* (London: Jonathan Cape, 1951), p. 337.

on the railroad system in European U.S.S.R. (although official Soviet figures appear exaggerated): 40,000 miles of track, 13,000 bridges, and 4,100 stations were among the estimated material losses.[2] However, with the advance of the Red Army, railroad construction was carried out with speed so that by the end of 1945, track length exceeded that of 1940, if we include some 7,000 miles of new lines built in unoccupied U.S.S.R. Subsequent developments have included the construction of the southern Siberian railroad, which directly joins Novokuznetsk to Magnitogorsk. This link relieves the heavily burdened section of the Trans-Siberian between Novosibirsk and Chelyabinsk, which formerly carried great loads of ore (from Magnitogorsk) and coal (from Kuzbas). The long-projected Baikal-Amur railroad was to continue the south Siberian eastwards from Novokuznetsk along a track to the north of the Trans-Siberian via Ust Kut, Tyndinsky and Komsomolsk to Soviet Harbor. Since its construction involves costly engineering works through mountainous and undeveloped country, only sections at each end appear to have been built: to Ust Kut and from Komsomolsk to Soviet Harbor. Current plans include the conversion of the railroads to electric and diesel traction. The electrified track in 1965 should treble the 1958 length. The manufacture of steam engines was stopped in 1956, and that of diesel and electric locomotives is being stepped up. The Trans-Siberian is now electrified as far east as Irkutsk, and the lines from Moscow to Leningrad and from Moscow to the Donbas and the Caucasus were to be electrified during 1962. Already by the end of 1960, 43 per cent of the freight was being hauled by electric and diesel locomotives, as compared with only 2.1 per cent in 1940, the 1965 target has been set at 85 per cent. Freight trains, with improved rolling stock, now carry even heavier loads at higher speeds. With 50- to 60-ton, four-axle freight cars, they can now carry about 4,000 to 6,000 tons, although the average load is nearer to 2,000 tons.

As the volume of freight increases in step with industrial expan-

[2] *Forty Years of Soviet Power in Facts and Figures,* Foreign Languages Publishing House (Moscow: 1958), p. 207.

sion and the growth of the urban population, the burden continues to fall on the railroads to the extent of 80 per cent in 1960. Of this freight, coal remains the chief item, accounting in 1956 for 30 per cent, despite the policy of developing many regional fields. The haulage of coal over long distances by steam-powered locomotives, which consume part of the load in transit, is a practice that is being steadily abandoned. The aim is to replace steam power completely by electric, diesel, and gas-turbine traction, as well as to reduce the direct consumption of coal through the greater use of electricity, oil, and natural gas. The other major items of freight, apart from machinery and equipment, are timber (7 per cent), ores (6 to 7 per cent), oil (over 6 per cent), iron and steel, including scrap (5 to 6 per cent), grain (over 5 per cent), and textile fibers. The 1959-1965 plan envisages some relief for the railroads which appears necessary: the freight density per mile of track is more than three times the United States average. One helpful development is the extension of pipelines for petroleum, a program limited only by the rate at which tubes can be produced. These already reach Omsk from the Volga-Ural field and are being continued to Irkutsk. Other pipes already supply Donbas (from Baku), Orsk (from Guriev, a new Soviet seaport on the north Caspian), Moscow (from the Volga-Ural field), and Ashkhabad, capital of Turkmen, from Krasnovodsk on the Caspian coast. Other pipeline projects include the supply of Volga-Ural oil to East Germany, Poland, Czechoslovakia, Hungary, and Bulgaria. The pipelines will terminate at Bratislava (Czechoslovakia) and Frankfort-on-Oder in Eastern Germany; works to this end began late in 1960.

INLAND WATERWAYS

Although inland waterways have more than doubled in length during the Soviet period—from 40,000 miles in 1913 to 85,000 in 1960—and carry a very much greater volume of freight, their relative importance has declined and continues to decline. This has not been officially desired. Indeed, considerable investment has been made in canal construction, river improvement, and the provision of ships and port facilities. On strictly economic ground, too, it has been argued that this capital would have been more profitably allocated to the railroads. Among Soviet canal constructions are the Baltic-White Sea canal which, making use of lakes Ladoga and Onega, links Leningrad to the White Sea; and the Volga-Don canal, a substantial engineering feat, which gives Volgograd and other Volga cities direct water access to the Donbas. Inland water transport suffers certain marked disadvantages, such as slowness, closure through the winter freeze and spring floods and, in the case of the rivers, a rigidly set course which often cuts across the required direction of traffic. At best, as in the southerly regions, the rivers are open for eight or nine months, while in the north, as in Siberia, navigation may be reduced downstream to as little as three months of the year. Another economic drawback is that the flow of traffic up and downstream is markedly uneven. Thus whereas the Volga and the Moskva have much more upstream than downstream freight, the position is reversed for the Neva, the North Dvina, and the Kama. The landlocked Caspian basin, with its railhead ports at Baku (Azerbaidzhan), Guriev (Kazakhstan), Makhachkala (Dagestan), and Krasnovodsk (Turkmen) may be regarded as an internal waterway. Contributing much to interregional relationships, it leads also to north Iranian ports. Lake Aral, like the Caspian, is little affected by winter freezing, and it assists regional traffic, as do many other lakes and many large reservoirs, such as those created above Rybinsk and Kuibyshev to serve hydroelectric installations.

The heaviest traffic on inland waterways is in lumber; in lesser volume, we can list petroleum, mineral building materials, grain, fish, salt, and coal. Additionally, the river routes service passengers, sometimes in diesel-electric ships, but more often in river buses. However, the people using this mode constitute only about 5 per cent of those who travel by rail. The Volga is without rival as a freight carrier, since it leads to Moscow, which, as a port of five seas, can be reached by waterways from the Baltic, White, Caspian, Black, and Azov seas. The great Siberian rivers, flowing through vast forested regions of scanty settlement, offer enormous lengths of navigation that is restricted to certain seasons. The largest volume of freight, lumber, is downstream, notably from Port Igarka on the Lower Yenisei. The northward-flowing Amu Darya and the eastward-flowing Amur are well used: the latter gives access for about half the year from the seaport of Nikolaevsk to Komsomolsk, Khabarovsk, and Blagoveshchensk.

MARITIME TRANSPORT

Coastwise traffic. The continental scale of the U.S.S.R. and the rigors of climate, most acutely felt in the northern and Far Eastern seas, combine to reduce the facility of coastwise navigation. While in this respect the U.S.S.R. is comparable with North America, there is no Panama Canal to shorten voyages between the Atlantic and the Pacific coasts. The Azov, Black, and Caspian seas are the most useful, carrying, for example, Georgian manganese from Poti, Donbas coal from Zhdanov to Kerch, and grain from Rostov to the South Caucasus. On the other hand, the Black Sea gives access to the navigable Danube along which are situated the Soviet satellites of Rumania, Bulgaria, Hungary, and Czechoslovakia, as well as Yugoslavia. With ports as far west as Kaliningrad, the U.S.S.R. can use the Baltic through all of the year for shipments between the northwest region of the R.S.F.S.R. centered on Leningrad and the Baltic republics. The value of the Baltic-White Sea canal, which involves a flight of locks, is much reduced by the winter freeze. Similarly, the local Pacific waters of the Far East offer shipping seasonal facilities only, although new ports have been built, notably Nagaevo (latitude 60°N.) and Soviet Harbor. Fortunately, Vladivostok is kept open virtually all through the year by icebreakers.

Soviet success in opening up the roundabout or northern sea route which extends for 7,000 statute miles between Archangel and Vladivostok has aroused considerable interest. While this route seeks to take advantage of the shortened distance in the north between Soviet eastern and western territories, which are otherwise related by sea by the longer route through the Suez Canal, it has been made practicable only after very considerable and costly scientific and technological effort. The local seas off the Siberian coast are open for two months east of Cape Chelyushkin, two to two and one-half months in the Kara Sea, and three and one-half months in the Barents Sea. This handicap requires organization necessary to make them serviceable for through shipments. Already before World War II it was claimed that the northern sea route functioned as a normal commercial route and that its ships were fueled by Arctic coal. Provision for the route has included the setting up of Arctic weather and radio stations; the development of a number of small ports of call, such as Anderma, Dikson, Nordvik, Tiksi, Ambarchik, Providence Bay, and Petropavlovsk (in Kamchatka); and the use of seaplanes for prospecting ahead of convoys, of icebreakers for clearing sea lanes. The route is very much an internal waterway for the U.S.S.R., although the possibility exists of increasing overseas shipments of lumber brought down in summer by the great rivers of Lena, Yenisei, and Irtysh. It can also serve the numerous mining enterprises dotted along the Siberian coast and located inland: coal, oil, salt, gold, tin and nickel. Specific operations of the route are concealed, but they may include the interchange of icebreakers, submarines, and other small naval vessels between the Atlantic and Pacific. Clearly, while the U.S.S.R. can justly feel pride in this Arctic achievement, the labors involved cannot claim to have yielded a commensurate economic return.

Overseas traffic. The U.S.S.R.'s share of world trade is little more than 3 per cent. However, overseas trade, while not large, is steadily increasing, and its sea-going merchant fleet has had to be supplemented by a similar tonnage of chartered ships. This trade is largely in such bulk goods as equipment, oil, timber, ores, and coal and serves markets in Africa, Asia, and Cuba as well as those nearer to home. The doubling of sea-going tonnage is an aim in the current plan by the provision of new, fast cargo vessels of 5,000 to 10,000-ton displacement, tankers of 20,000 and 30,000 tons, and refrigeration and whaling ships.

ROAD TRANSPORT

Although road transport is scheduled to double during the 1958-1965 plan period, it contributes relatively little to the economy. Certainly the great distances, the lack of local road-building materials in many areas, and the effects of snow, frost, and flood make road building and maintenance costly. Even so, the mileage of hard-surface roads in 1956 was 134,000 (nine times that of 1913), but their purpose is mainly for the local movement of passengers and freight. Although more than half of the automobiles are privately owned, emphasis is put on public transport services, especially those of buses, trolley buses and trams that ply within and between the towns. The production of trucks, motor cars, motorcycles, scooters, and bicycles is fast increasing. But in road transport development, especially in the manufacture of privately owned vehicles, the U.S.S.R. lags far behind the western countries. Roads have been wholly or partially built in certain mountainous parts of the country lacking railroads. Examples are those connecting Yakutsk in Eastern Siberia to the coast at Okhotsk and Ayan and to Tyndinsky (a railhead for the Trans-Siberian), and that in Central Asia from Osh across the Pamir to Khorog. Plans include motor roads from Moscow to Brest Litovsk via Minsk and to Kiev, Kharkov, and Rostov on the Don River. But even the far-reaching plans for 1980 do not envisage private motoring in the western way, which is considered wasteful as well as individualistic. The 1980 plan, however, includes the provision of 15 million cars for hire.

TRAVEL BY AIR

By 1956 air transport had made considerable strides from the position reached in 1940. Passenger traffic had grown 18 times, mail transport 9 times, and freight 14 times. While air freight is particularly economical for carrying such commodities as platinum, gold, and diamonds, which generally are produced in areas far from the railroad, the prime value in the Soviet Union is for transporting mail, personnel, and supplies to such remote places as Arctic stations and mining camps. Regular services connect the principal towns of the Union as well as many European and Asiatic countries. Only 10 to 12 hours in the air were needed in 1956 to fly between the outer western and eastern borders of the Union. Aeroflot possesses high-speed jet and turbo-prop aircraft, such as the TU-104, which carries 80 to 120 passengers at speeds up to 625 mph., and the TU-114, which can carry 170 passengers and fly 6,000 miles nonstop in eight and one-half hours.[3] Auxiliary uses of aircraft include forest patrols, ambulance service, aerial mapping, prospecting, and chemical spraying.

8 *The Frontiers and Boundaries of the U.S.S.R.*

WE noted in Chapter 3 how Russia began as Muscovy and grew around a small territorial core set within the mixed forests of the Great Russian lowland by a process of expansion outward into zones of contrasting character: coniferous forests and tundra, wooded and grass steppes, and even mountains and deserts. The limits which contained Russia at different periods depended mainly on its political and military strength in relation to that of its neighbors, who were at times strengthened by co-operation against it. Insofar as it was possible to conceive of rational and justifiable boundaries to Russia, these rested on the geographical distribution of Russians proper—i.e., those of Great Russian speech. In an area of wide lowlands, virtually lacking in such physical features as imposed convenient and defensible borders, Russia's rulers had to extend as and where they could, the better to safeguard

[3] The new Ilyushin-62 jet airliner designed for the Atlantic trade made its first trip from Moscow to Tallin (Estonia) in October 1962.

their own areas of settlement. As Russia's political organization and military power grew, the country expanded not only into areas of White Russian and Ukrainian settlement but also into colonial regions, notably Siberia and Kazakhstan. Imperialistic conquests took the tsars into Central Asia, South Caucasus, and Finland. The term "Russian Empire" rightly characterized the extensive territorial heritage of the tsars; the U.S.S.R., in contrast, started its career within restricted boundaries imposed from outside on a country defeated in war and disorganized within.

The rulers of the U.S.S.R. rationalized this situation by declaring loudly that they had no colonies and indeed condemned imperialistic systems as a means of capitalistic exploitation. Yet as it grew stronger and as opportunity arose, both before it entered World War II (in June 1941) and after it, the U.S.S.R resorted to a policy of territorial expansion which brought its limits broadly comparable to those of Russia in 1913. Moreover, it has been at pains to organize many neighboring countries, so far as it could, in a way conducive to its own political, defensive, and economic interests. In order fully to understand the U.S.S.R. of today, it is thus necessary to look attentively at both its frontiers and its boundaries, remembering that such geographical considerations are of equal importance in matters of defense, foreign policy, and international politics generally.

TERRITORIAL EXPANSION OF THE U.S.S.R.

By the end of World War II, the U.S.S.R. had increased its territory by about 3 per cent. This small proportion amounted to 273,000 square miles, of which more than two-thirds were won in Europe. Accessions there were equivalent to an area larger than California's and were obtained by the incorporation of three formerly independent states—the Baltic republics of Lithuania, Latvia, and Estonia—and by the annexation of borderlands from no less than six other states. In Asia, territorial gains were less, but they included the former protectorate of Tannu-Tuva, now organized as the Tuvan A.S.S.R., and southern Sakhalin and the Kurile Islands from

Japan. These additions of territory brought 23 million more
under the U.S.S.R.'s direct rule and added nearly 15 per cent to its
manpower, which had been depleted through war. Other interesting geographical results were that the U.S.S.R. shortened its boundaries in Europe, strengthened its position on the Baltic Sea, reached
to the delta of the Danube River, and made direct contact with
three more European neighbors—Norway, Czechoslovakia, and
Hungary—from which it had been formerly separated by Finnish,
Polish, and Rumanian territory, respectively. In the Far East, because of territorial acquisitions, the U.S.S.R. has been able to regard
the Okhotsk Sea as virtually a Soviet lake.

THE U.S.S.R.'S LIMITS AND NEIGHBORS IN EUROPE

The land and sea boundaries of the U.S.S.R. extend for about
33,000 miles. The greater part are made up of coastlines on the
Arctic Ocean, the Pacific Ocean and the Baltic, Black, and Caspian
seas, beyond which it exercises sovereignty over territorial seas of
a breadth of 12 miles. Of the U.S.S.R.'s land boundaries, approxi-
mately 10,000 miles in length, about 2,000 miles delimit its territory
in Europe against six neighbors—Norway, Finland, Poland, Czechoslovakia, Hungary, and Rumania. These European boundaries re-
flect the U.S.S.R.'s victory over Germany and its allies in World
War II and project the U.S.S.R. westward into the politically un-
stable zone of east-central Europe. This area, formerly known as the
Shatter Zone,[1] consisted during the interwar years of 1919-1938 of
a tier of states oriented to the West and designed above all to
separate Russia from Germany.

Mainly, though not exactly, the U.S.S.R.'s post-1945 boundaries in
Europe mark its recovery of former territories of the Russian Empire
which had been lost during World War I. These losses the new
Bolshevik rulers of Russia had no other choice than to accept. If the

[1] W. G. East, "The Concept and Political Status of the Shatter Zone," *Geographical Essays on Eastern Europe,* edited by N. J. G. Pounds, Indiana University Publications, vol. 24 (Bloomington); and Mouton & Co. (The Hague),
1961, pp. 1-27.

creation of new, independent, national states on their western border freed them from certain immediate difficulties, nevertheless it seriously weakened them for defense, especially in the north. Also, it deprived them of some good agricultural lands, especially in the south.

Soviet territorial gains in the north. The independent Republic of Finland, oriented to the western countries, enjoyed an open all-year seaport on the Barents Sea at Petsamo and worked the nickel deposits nearby. Also, a southern boundary passed across Lake Ladoga to the Gulf of Finland across the narrow Karelian Isthmus, only about 30 miles wide, north of Leningrad. The U.S.S.R. had been left in fact with only one outlet to the Baltic, at Leningrad. This large city of over three million inhabitants, which accounted for about one-eighth of the whole of Soviet industrial output, was left highly vulnerable to any attack launched from either Finnish territory to the north or Estonian territory to the west. While Stalin had nothing to fear from either of these small nations, he calculated that either or both might become a base or means of approach for a powerful enemy. This consideration explains the Soviet attack on Finland in November 1939 and the attempt, not immediately successful, to break the Mannerheim Line across the Karelian Isthmus. It explains, too, why the U.S.S.R. set up along the border with Finland the Karelian-Finnish A.S.S.R., which was upgraded in 1940 as the Karelian S.S.R., although its population in 1939, including immigrant Russians, was only 600,000. Actuated in part by defense considerations but also by the desire to recover former Russian provinces, the U.S.S.R. was able, under the Russo-German Pact of 1939 (i.e., before Hitler launched his attack on the Union), to occupy the independent republics of Lithuania, Latvia, and Estonia. Plebiscites held in these countries in 1940, while they were under the occupation of the Red Army, were reported to have demonstrated the people's desire to join the U.S.S.R. as constituent republics. As such, they were incorporated, and so they remain.

After fighting two wars with Finland, the U.S.S.R. was able to make substantial gains of territory and to secure improved boundaries. In the extreme north, by annexing the area that included the nickel deposits of Petsamo (renamed Pechenga), it deprived Finland of its Arctic outlet and made direct contact with Norway's province of Finnmark. Further south, the Karelian-Finnish S.S.R. was expanded at the expense of Finland. The most southerly section of the Soviet-Finnish boundary was moved north to give the U.S.S.R. control of the whole of Lake Ladoga and of the Karelian Isthmus, together with the seaport of Vyborg (in Finnish, Vipurii). These losses of territory involved Finland in the resettlement of 400,000 Finns who chose to leave the ceded areas; Finland, too, was required to pay heavy reparations to the U.S.S.R. and to orient its trade to that country. Yet the U.S.S.R. showed no inclination to incorporate Finland into the Union as it did with the other Baltic states, although Finland had been part of the Russian Empire between 1809 and 1917.

One other Soviet acquisition in the north was the northern section of East Prussia, a detached part of Germany which had been conquered and colonized by the Teutonic Knights as long as the thirteenth century. This accession gave the U.S.S.R. control of Königsberg (now Kaliningrad), a westerly seaport in the Baltic; the larger, remaining part of East Prussia was handed over to Poland. This bold and novel change effaced from the map an area of Germany which, during the interwar years, had been separated from its body by the Polish Corridor to the Baltic Sea.

Soviet territorial gains in the west. Between Lithuania and the Carpathian Mountains, the U.S.S.R. advanced its boundary about 150 miles to the west by the annexation of former parts of Poland, Czechoslovakia, and Rumania. It should be recalled that eighteenth-century Poland had been partitioned among its three powerful neighbors; that the small kingdom of Poland around Warsaw, which had been created after the Napoleonic Wars, had passed to the tsar as king and had thus become virtually a province of the Russian Empire; and that after World War I the western powers had set up an independent Polish republic. This republic took advantage of the weakness of the new Bolshevik government to expand its territories substantially to the east into regions which were in no sense clearly and unmistakably Polish. Indeed, although the population of eastern Poland, largely of poor peasants, was mixed ethnographically, the largest elements making up about two-thirds of the total were White Russians and Ukrainians.

To the Soviet Union these lands were known as Russia's western lands and their recovery was based on nationality grounds. Actually, the new Soviet-Polish boundary, as defined by the Potsdam Agreement, accorded closely to the Curzon Line, a Russo-Polish boundary proposed in 1920 which took account of the distribution of the nationalities. The proportion of Poles in these annexed territories has been heavily debated, but it was probably not much in excess of 20 per cent; also, there had been a strong minority of Jews in the towns before Hitler's purge. Although the recovered western lands offered no substantial industrial resources and consisted chiefly of agricultural lands in need of development—including the western part of the Pripet Marshes—they contained also two important railroad junctions at Brest Litovsk and Lvov. Main lines converge on these towns, respectively, from Moscow and Odessa and they both continue to Berlin, the first through Warsaw and the second by way of Krakow and Wroclaw. Both the Byelorussian and Ukrainian S.S.R.'s were enlarged by these accessions from Poland, which were divided administratively into oblasts.

On similar ethnographic ground, the U.S.S.R. annexed from Hungary the region between the Carpathian watershed and the Upper Tisza River, which the Hungarians called Ruthenia although to the Russians it was known as Sub-Carpathian Russia or as Carpatho-Ukraine. Since its population of shepherds and peasants, numbering about 750,000, was largely of Ukrainian descent, the U.S.S.R. was able to present its annexation as the liberation of brothers from alien rule. Here again this area was more interesting strategically than economically, for across this sector of the Carpathians pass railways and roads linking the Galicia plateau to the Hungarian basin. It had formed the most easterly projection of the Czechoslovakian republic which was created after World War I, although Hitler had returned it to the Hungarian kingdom of which it had been a part. Also, Ruthenia was added to the Ukraine S.S.R., causing the U.S.S.R. to border Hungary directly. The value of, and need for, this direct route were illustrated when used by the Red Army in quelling the Hungarian revolt of 1956. The tsar's army had also used it to overthrow the Hungarian Revolution of 1849.

The U.S.S.R. made territorial claims on Rumania, too. The territories annexed were Bessarabia, which lies between the Prut River and the Kilia channel of the Danube delta to the west and the Dniester River to the east; and Bukovina, a Carpathian upland of beechwood forests which adjoined it to the north. These two areas were parts of the Rumanian kingdom between the wars, but their populations were mixed—mainly a combination of Rumanians, Ukrainians, and Jews. Historically, their political associations were various. In 1775 Bukovina, which was part of the Ottoman Empire, was incorporated into the Hungarian kingdom, while Bessarabia, which was also part of that empire and rather more than half Rumanian in population, had been ceded to Russia in 1812—to be lost only in 1919 when the Rumanian kingdom was enlarged. The U.S.S.R. had clearly prepared for its eventual incorporation by creating the small Moldavian A.S.S.R. in 1933, although Moldavians—i.e., those of Rumanian speech akin to the more numerous Moldavians within Rumania—were only about one-third of its population. The larger part of Bessarabia was added to the Moldavian A.S.S.R., which was raised to the status of a Union republic (S.S.R.) in 1940. Bukovina and the coastal lowlands of Bessarabia were added to the Ukraine which, as a result of all its territorial gains, extended west to beyond the northern Carpathians and to the Danube delta.

The U.S.S.R.'s claims on Rumania rested on no strong ethnographic ground; they were not, however, without economic interest. Bessarabia continues westward the Ukrainian steppe and provides productive arable land for mixed farming, which yields a useful surplus of grain and animal products. The U.S.S.R. also took advantage of the fact that it had become one of the many states which reach or lie astride the Danube River, by ending the international regime which governed its use for the commerce of all nations.[2]

The U.S.S.R.'s neighbors in Europe. Despite its many territorial gains, the U.S.S.R.'s western limits do not reach as far west as did those of the Russian Empire in 1913 because that included the Polish kingdom. However, it is more realistic to note how the U.S.S.R., through the presence of the Red Army, was able to create beyond its own boundaries dependent states under Communist regimes in east-central Europe. Stalin's policy in this respect may be seen as primarily aimed at increasing Soviet defensive strength in a way natural enough to a continental power. It compares and contrasts with the policy of the United States in seeking defense at long range by the creation of aero-naval bases around the periphery of the Soviet Union. The result of this policy was to reverse that which had been applied by the western powers after World War I and to secure for the U.S.S.R. a borderland of countries which, despite their strong national characters, could be controlled by Moscow and induced to share in its political, social, and economic plans.

The U.S.S.R.'s European neighbors form part of a zone of political instability—a political shatter zone where feelings between nations were strong, national populations intermingled, cultural levels uneven, and the social structure more Russian or even Asiatic than western. In imposing its will on the nations of this zone, the U.S.S.R. has in some measure succeeded in impressing on them its own political, social, and economic pattern and has given the zone a certain stability as part of its empire. Yet the U.S.S.R.'s relationship to the member states of this zone is not uniform, although much has been done to bring them together under Moscow's leadership, notably for economic co-operation by the Council for Mutual Economic Aid (1949) and for defense by the Warsaw Pact (1955).

[2] See W. G. East and A. E. Moodie (eds.), *The Changing World: Studies in Political Geography* (Yonkers-on-Hudson, N.Y.: The World Book Co., and London: G. Harrap & Co., 1956), p. 422.

In particular, the U.S.S.R. has left Finland relatively free to enjoy a western form of democratic government, although by treaty it can maintain only such military forces as are required to preserve internal order. While Finland was allowed even to join the European Free Trade Association, it necessarily accords a most favored nation position to its mighty neighbor. The position of Yugoslavia, too, remains anomalous. Marshal Tito, who won his country's loyalty independently of Moscow, has succeeded in deviating along a line of national communism, and adopts for Yugoslavia the posture of an uncommitted state. Poland, in contrast, stands closely aligned with Moscow within new limits (expanded at the expense of Germany), for the continuance of which it must depend on the U.S.S.R. Even so, as a result of the popular disorders of 1956, Poland won the right to give consent to Soviet troop movements in Poland and to subject Soviet troops to Polish courts. It has been able to avoid the establishment of the Soviet collective-farm system in favor of its own co-operative system and, due to Khrushchev's relaxation of the rigidities of Stalinism, has won a little freedom for national maneuvers. Czechoslovakia, Hungary, Rumania, and Bulgaria broadly conform to the pattern of satellite states oriented now to the East in regard to their economic, political, and defense policies.

Eastern Germany, organized as the German Democratic Republic, together with the Soviet Zone of Berlin, remains in colonial dependence on the U.S.S.R. Its status is a political embarrassment to Moscow, yet the area is economically the most important of the Union's satellites. The dictatorship of the Stalinist Ulbricht persists, and union between the German Democratic Republic and the German Federal Republic is precluded because of the sharp and fundamental differences dividing the U.S.S.R. and the western powers. Khrushchev has said that he preferred the certainty of having 20 million Germans with him to the possibility of having 70 million neutralized Germans against him.

In short, the Soviet empire in Europe extends measurably beyond the U.S.S.R.'s own western boundaries, and the world has learned again how Soviet communism can succeed when the Red Army is r near at hand. The solution imposed on east-central Europe by Stalin has proved disadvantageous to the West in several ways: strategically, by bringing the U.S.S.R.'s armed forces far to the west; politically, by breaking former ties; and economically, by reducing to a minimum former commercial relationships with countries that were largely western in outlook. On the other hand, the U.S.S.R. has given to the nations of the shatter zone a certain stability and economic leadership that they needed. Further, since the U.S.S.R. provides an insatiable market, renders financial assistance to its satellites, and supplies them with such useful trade commodities as petroleum and raw cotton, their close association with the Union may be regarded as wholly reasonable on both geographical and economic grounds.

THE U.S.S.R.'S FRONTIERS IN ASIA

The Asian frontiers of the Soviet Union stretch latitudinally for about 8,000 miles and, in contrast to those in Europe, lie mostly within a country of separative character that includes areas of scanty settlement, mountains, and high arid plateaus. In the west, the Soviet borders impinge on the Middle East, a region of high geopolitical tension where formerly the United Kingdom and France held a controlling position. Today, however, many of the countries of this region strike xenophobic and uncommitted attitudes towards both the U.S.S.R. and the western powers, each of which holds or seeks to hold vantage points. Farther east, the U.S.S.R. borders the two buffer states of Iran and Afghanistan, which bar its direct path to the Indian Ocean. Thereafter, for thousands of miles, except where its satellite Mongolia is interposed, the U.S.S.R.'s territories and interests meet those of China. With this country, the U.S.S.R. has been compelled to make compromises not wholly to its taste in order to achieve the considerable benefits of co-operation with a revolutionary state of outsize demographic scale. Finally, in the eastern area, where the U.S.S.R. is next to North Korea as well as China, it borders (at great distance from its main bases) another region of geopolitical tension—the Far East.

The Soviet border in the Middle East. Turkey, like the U.S.S.R., emerged as a republic after World War I and adopted a neutral position during World War II. In its defensive posture towards its great neighbor, whose territories adjoin its own in a mountainous region between the Black and Caspian seas, it has shown remarkable consistency. It is aware that the U.S.S.R. has made claims to border areas around Kars and Ardahan and that the settlement of Armenians alike in Soviet South Caucasus and in northeastern Turkey can be used to foment difficulties. Further, as guardian of the Turkish straits, Turkey controls access between the Black Sea, where the U.S.S.R. is navally dominant, and the Mediterranean, which is under NATO control. Turkey sought and received military and financial aid from the United States and has repaid this by presenting NATO with a strong sector on its right flank. In short, Soviet policy has achieved no successes in its relations with Turkey.

Similarly, the boundaries between the U.S.S.R. and both Iran and Afghanistan have proved stable. In earlier years Russia and the United Kingdom showed comparable interest in these two politically weak countries of mountainous topography, backward economies, yet interesting locations. Russia naturally was interested in insuring that they did not prove dangerous to its South Caucasian and Central Asian dependencies. Similarly Britain, interested in defending India, wished to insure that a major power like Russia, by controlling Iran and Afghanistan, did not establish itself on the Indian Ocean. Such strategical interests, related to unchanging facts of location, necessarily persist. The U.S.S.R. has not managed to bring about, as in east-central Europe, Communist regimes that would tie these Moslem countries firmly to the Communist bloc. Accordingly, it has been at pains to win the good will of the Iranians and Afghans by propaganda, official visits, trade agreements, ruble credits, and such spectacular construction works as the one which brought electricity to Kabul. Of course, the United States and the other major western powers have shown in similar ways their desire to maintain the political *status quo.*

The Sino-Soviet border. Here within a broad borderland, set mostly remote from the oceans and in arid, mountainous, and high plateau country, the Russian Empire, as it expanded, pressed into country which had formed outer parts of the Chinese Empire in the days of its greatest extent. It was Russia's conquest of Siberia in the seventeenth century and of the Kazakh steppes in the eighteenth century that first brought it to the approaches to Sinkiang and Mongolia, which were Chinese by conquest rather than by settlement. As Chinese power weakened seriously in the latter half of the nineteenth century, Russia naturally sought to strengthen its defensive position by penetrating into, and seeking to dominate, Sinkiang, Tannu-Tuva, Outer Mongolia and Manchuria; the last, south of the Amur River, particularly tempted the Russians because of its potential wealth as a granary and workshop, and because of the usefulness of its warm-water ports. While the U.S.S.R. condemned the former Russian imperialism and renounced its rights in Manchuria, it was well aware that stabilization was necessary in this frontier of tension. As a precaution, it maintained strong local forces for defense against Japan, which dominated China in the 1930's.

World War II ended Japan's territorial hold on China, and the triumph of Communist forces there in 1949 completely transformed what had long been a frontier of separation and of tension into one of contact and co-operation. Certainly, Stalin claimed a high price at Yalta for his share—a six weeks' campaign—in the overthrow of Japan. His demands included south Sakhalin and the Kurile Islands, which the tsars had formerly held, and also a lease of Port Arthur for a naval base, the internationalization of the commercial port of Dairen, and a privileged position in Manchuria from which he carried off, as war booty, much industrial equipment. Further, the U.S.S.R. absorbed the Tannu-Tuva protectorate, which contains headwaters of the Yenisei River; and controlled Outer Mongolia, which as early as 1921 had been organized as the Mongolian People's Republic, was later linked by railway to the Trans-Siberian, and was actively engaged in developing neighboring parts of Sinkiang.

Sino-Soviet friendship and co-operation, heralded by the Sino-Soviet treaty of 1950, brought further remarkable changes in that the

U.S.S.R. freely yielded up to its fellow Communist neighbor its rights in Manchuria, as well as in Sinkiang. Mongolia remains a Soviet satellite, but the railway has been extended to give access to Peking, and thus to bring Chinese settlers to Ulan Bator, the Mongolian capital. Further, to make the Jade Gate to China more useful, a railway is being constructed from Alma Ata, capital of Soviet Kazakhstan, across Sinkiang to link with Peking. Hence, under relatively stable conditions, the considerable mineral resources of Sinkiang are being developed by China. Manchuria has become increasingly its chief workshop and a provider of surplus foodstuffs, while Mongolia would appear prosperous with its large livestock resources and successful conversion to the Soviet system. Beyond doubt, great economic and demographic changes will be taking place during the decades ahead in these vast inner Asian countries, which were formerly mere pawns in the imperialist game.[3] In this context one should also recall Soviet large-scale industrial developments near the Sino-Soviet border in Eastern Siberia (see above, p. 79).

CONCLUSION

The U.S.S.R. clearly exploited with success the chances offered by the defeat of Hitler's Germany and the Japanese Empire in World War II and has almost assumed the territorial extent of the tsarist empire. The stabilization effected along its long border with China contrasts with the state of tension which continues on its European border and with the uneasy geopolitical situation which persists in the Middle East. It should be recognized that powerful states naturally seek to strengthen themselves around their peripheries, and that this strengthening has usually meant either territorial expansion or other means of control. It should be noted, however, as an unusual case, that the U.S.S.R. actually made substantial concessions to China. The foregoing review of the frontiers of the Soviet Union

[3] Interested readers may be referred to the Searchlight Book, W. A. Douglas Jackson, *Russo-Chinese Borderlands* (Princeton, N.J.: D. Van Nostrand Company, Inc., 1962).

has seemed worthwhile, if only because herein lies one source of Soviet strength: the U.S.S.R., beyond its own linear boundaries, can operate by devious means among peoples little able to resist its wiles in Europe and Asia alike.

9   *The Status of the U.S.S.R.*
           in the World

In previous chapters, we have outlined the salient features of the Soviet land and peoples and showed how the U.S.S.R., as heir to the Russian Empire, has been vigorously exploiting its natural resources, industrializing the economy, and transforming society. The advent of the Soviet Union had been greeted with dismay in the western world, for it appeared to indicate a decline of civilized ways and to usher in a period of revolutionary terror. To Dr. Isaiah Bowman,[1] a detached observer with insight and a high degree of objectivity, Bolshevism meant "a step backward toward the barbarism of earlier times." Suspicion and fear of, and aversion to Soviet ideology and methods, have persisted widely, although doubts of whether the Soviet system could work effectively in the country of its birth have been dispelled. The world has witnessed the U.S.S.R.'s growing strength and notes the successes which it achieved, first in the defeat of Hitler's Germany, and second in technological, economic, and international fields. Whereas during the two decades between the world wars, the U.S.S.R. stood largely aloof from the rest of the world, being deeply involved in its own internal problems of political integration and economic organization, it has now,

[1] Isaiah Bowman, *The New World: Problems in Political Geography* (Yonkers-on-Hudson, The World Book Co., 1921; and London: George G. Harrap & Co., 1922), p. 388.

since 1945, emerged conscious of its strength, stability, and great-power status. Since it is now one of only two great powers, it is clearly determined to play a commensurate part in world affairs.

It should not be forgotten that Russia, already 150 years ago, occupied a central position on the world stage. The Russia of Tsar Alexander I in 1807, which appeared then to be dividing not only Europe but lands overseas between itself and the Emperor Napoleon of France, and the Russia of 1812-1815, which took a leading part in his defeat and in the resettlement of Europe afterwards, was clearly one of several powers to be reckoned with. Its subsequent political weakness grew out of its own social and economic backwardness which was the more emphasized as Britain, France, and Germany in turn advanced economically as a result of the Industrial Revolution. The Bolshevik Revolution began to release and then to harness the energy of the Russian and other Soviet peoples towards the deliberate enhancement of state power based on the sinews of modern industry. No diversion or dissipation of effort merely to make life easier for the Soviet individual has been allowed measurably to weaken the prime objective: the building of the U.S.S.R. as a fortress safe from attack and strong enough to win or woo adherents beyond its borders to its own ideology. And inside the Union, and to some extent beyond it, the Communist party provided a trained elite of leaders fitted to carry out Soviet policy as this was elaborated at the center.

SOVIET MILITARY STATURE AND THE IDEOLOGICAL WEAPON

It is important to realize that, ideology apart, the Soviet Union emerged from World War II as a great military power in Eurasia: only its lack of atomic bombs, which had already impressed Stalin, limited its military ascendancy there. Its two principal enemies, Germany and Japan, were stricken, and its Asiatic flank was further strengthened by the triumph of Communist forces in mainland China with which it made a treaty of friendship and mutual defense in 1950. Hitler's wayward policy, in defiance of the teaching of

German strategists, of involving his country in a war on two flanks, saved the U.S.S.R. from its greatest danger, that of being destroyed in a war waged alone against Germany. The armed forces of the U.S.S.R.—which are now developed for warfare alike on land, in the air, and at sea and are equipped with ever more destructive weapons —this, rather than Soviet ideology, is the principal sobering fact which explains Soviet great-power status.

Its allies and satellites in Europe and Asia provide defensive insulation to its own territory, although they are not wholly factors of strength. Yugoslavia succeeded in deviating along an independent line of national socialism. The 1953 rising in Eastern Germany and the 1956 rebellions in Hungary and Poland showed how much their Communist regimes depended on the military and economic support of Moscow. More recently, too, Albania has swerved from Moscow's leadership in favor of Peking's. The Warsaw Pact of 1955 which, in reaction to the launching of NATO, united for defense the U.S.S.R. and its European satellites, should be presumed to enjoy broadly similar solidarity if only because powerful Soviet forces are near at hand, including the 22 divisions of the Red Army which support Herr Ulbricht's dictatorship in Eastern Germany. Yet allies and satellites involve the U.S.S.R. in considerable difficulties. Khrushchev found it advisable to make concessions to the Poles relevant to the movements, for example, of Soviet troops along his so-called lines of communication to Berlin. Eastern Germany, including the Soviet sector of Berlin, has clearly presented bristling difficulties and international dangers.

Mainland China, more than three times as populous as the U.S.S.R. but at an early stage of its planned industrialization, is evidently no satellite of the U.S.S.R. At times, indeed, it is a considerable embarrassment. Certainly, the recent Indian conflict is a good example. It is fortunate that the U.S.S.R. has such a friend, for it thus faces continually the problem of having to reconcile a conflict of views and policies and cannot assume, unchallenged, the leadership of the Communist bloc. The ideological quarrel between Moscow and Albania illustrates the difficulties which arise—and incidentally deprives the U.S.S.R. of the control of a vantage point on the Mediterranean Sea. The Communist bloc, made up of the U.S.S.R. and China, together with the satellites of each—for China has its own satellites, notably North Korea and North Viet Nam—accounts for about one-third of mankind, but it is neither a single culture world nor a single unit in geopolitics.

Even though the status of the U.S.S.R. in the world rests primarily on its armed might backed by its industrial and technological potential, it owes something also to the powerful weapon of its ideology. Soviet communism has always offered its revolutionary message to the workers of the world regardless of the national divisions which persist, and it seeks by its efforts at home to show to what heights of material achievement a Soviet regime can reach stage by stage. Since capitalism in the western world refuses to collapse—and indeed shows renewed vigor as demonstrated in the Common Market countries—the U.S.S.R. has sought increasingly to challenge and, where possible, surpass it in the field of production. Powerful propaganda is directed by a variety of skillful means to suggest the superiority of the Soviet to the capitalist system in the belief that communism will eventually prevail in mere economic competition rather than as a result of war. The U.S.S.R. remains as ever hegemonic in its aspirations but shows readiness to adapt its methods according to its estimate of what advances can be made under the circumstances of the time. Propaganda provides one means of changing and shaping human minds and, insofar as it succeeds in ways adverse to western capitalism, it brings grist to the Soviet wheel.

THE U.S.S.R. AND THE HEARTLAND OF MACKINDER

Before exploring further the new Soviet bid to outdo the West in an economic, political, and psychological struggle waged within the framework of so-called peaceful coexistence, it is worth recalling how sharply the situation has changed since the years which immediately followed World War II. It was then envisaged that the Soviet Union and the United States might become involved in global war to determine which should master the world. Much interest was then aroused by the geopolitical analysis of Sir Halford Mackinder, which seemed to favor the Soviet chances. His basic thinking and writing in the field were done before the end of World War I but their relevance to the post-World War II international situation appeared almost uncanny.

The original purpose of his famous book[2] was to emphasize, for the benefit of the western peacemakers at the close of World War I, the danger to the peace of Europe and thus of the world, of a collision between the two military powers of Germany and Russia. To this end he argued the need for a separative tier of nation states in east-central Europe that could, with western support, insulate those two potentially dangerous states. Moreover, as a result of what appears a simple analysis, yet one well grounded alike on the facts of geography and of history, Mackinder attached remarkable importance to what he called the Heartland of the Old World Island. The latter consisted of the three continents of Europe, Asia and Africa, which contain over four-fifths of mankind, and the former—the Heartland—was a subcontinental region, lying east of the Volga, now made up of Soviet territory and of lands beyond it to the south. The Heartland, according to Mackinder, possessed enormous defensive strength, related to its physical geography—its vastness, its relative inaccessibility to the oceans, and its advantage in commanding interior lines of communication. Further, he believed that, if the Heartland was controlled by the state which ruled east Europe—roughly the area between the Volga and the present eastern limits of the German Federal Republic—such a state was well endowed and well poised to attempt military and, subsequently, political mastery of the world.

It is evident that the territorially expanded U.S.S.R. at the end of World War II ruled not only the east Europe of Mackinder, but also most of the Heartland. While it did not control Iran,

[2] Sir H. J. Mackinder, *Democratic Ideals and Reality* (London: Constable & Co., and New York: Henry Holt & Co., 1919; and London: Pelican Edition, 1944).

Trandate

Afghanistan, and Tibet, which were largely or wholly reckoned parts of the Heartland, it was fortuitously strengthened by the emergence of Communist China. Yet, although the dice seemed loaded in the U.S.S.R.'s favor, there were new considerations relevant to the balance of Soviet and American power which the Mackinder analysis had not—and could not have at the time—taken into account. For example, the United States' lead with the first atomic bombs, the opening up of the Arctic to air navigation, and the U.S.S.R.'s heavy task of rehabilitating its war-devastated areas are a few examples. The armaments race has, of course, continued at great cost, supporting the development on both sides of weapons of terrific power. Indeed it has been so successful as to reveal that a nuclear war even if won would yield to any aggressor dubious rewards obtained assuredly at immeasurable and clearly excessive cost. Further, if the U.S.S.R. were to engage in all-out modern war, it would more than jeopardize the great material achievements made since the revolution, as well as the current plans for ever-greater advances towards its Communist goal.

KHRUSHCHEV AT THE HELM

Hence the U.S.S.R., conscious of its strength and stability and mindful of the serious hazards of an all-out conflict with the western bloc led by the United States, has devised new external policies which, it estimates, may prove fruitful in the course of time. The newly found stability, following the period of collective leadership after Stalin's death in 1954, is a result of the remarkable political skill of Nikita Khrushchev. Using his close knowledge of Soviet institutions of government and of leading party personalities to swing policy away from the ruthlessness of Stalinism, he acquired for himself unchallenged leadership by the end of 1957.[3]

On the internal aspect of Khrushchev's success, only a few salient

[3] For an illuminating and concise account of how Khrushchev wrested control into his own hands and of his policy changes, see "Russia and the 22nd Congress," *Current Affairs Bulletin* (Sydney), January 29, 1962, vol. 29, no. 6.

points need be noted here. In March 1958, after removing Bulganin, he assumed the office of Chairman of the Council of Ministers, while retaining his key office as the first Secretary of the Communist Party's Central Committee. Leading Stalinists—Malenkov, Kaganovich, Shepilov, and Molotov—were removed from positions of power, as were such wartime generals as Bulganin, Voroshilov, and Zhukov (reputedly Stalin's ablest strategist). Internal difficulties, which included a few spontaneous strikes and certain nationalist deviations, as in Latvia and Azerbaidzhan, were effectively dealt with. Everyday living was made somewhat easier by ending the great arbitary powers formerly wielded by the secret police, expanding consumer industries, devolving the administrative control of industry to the major regions, increasing state prices for agricultural produce, and reducing working hours in factories to 40 hours a week. At the end of 1957 Khrushchev had managed to create a Presidium in which 10 of the 15 members belonged to his so-called "anti-Party group." During the two following years he restored powers to the Council of Ministers, of which he was Chairman. To stabilize and strengthen further the home front came the policy pronouncements of the Twenty-second Party Congress, which met at Moscow in 1961. These included above all the long-term plans for 1970 and 1980 which mark the transition from socialism to communism, from a situation where goods and services are distributed according to work done towards one where they are distributed according to need. It should be realized that individual needs are assessed by the policy-makers, not by the democratic principle that he who wears the shoe knows best where it pinches. The long-term plan made it clear that no withering away of the powers of centralized government is yet envisaged; that, while wages will increase considerably, they will remain widely unequal;[4] and that, even if 1980 goals are achieved, housing conditions will still fall far short of

---

[4] Yet this inequality of salaries and wages is already small compared with that in western Europe and the United States. Leaders in the arts and sciences, who are among the elite in the U.S.S.R., received in 1962 incomes reaching at most to $18,000 a year.

western standards. Broadly, it can be said that the lot of the Soviet citizen has greatly improved since the dark days of World War II and of the period of rehabilitation which followed it. He is offered, too, the triumphs of Soviet science and technology in the heavens, and doubtless the assurance that powerful means exist to preserve the Soviet system from possible external dangers. Although the cost of sputniks, cosmonauts, and armaments must be staggering (of course, the expense of the last item might well be reduced through international disarmament agreements), the Soviet economy can now presumably bear this strain and at the same time steadily increase living standards.

It is ironic that, although Khrushchev's de-Stalinization policy has brought stability and contentment to the U.S.S.R., it has aroused marked hostility in China and thus deprived him of the leadership of a solid Communist bloc to which he undoubtedly aspires. Therefore, since the Communist bloc is a house divided against itself, the Kremlin must tread warily where its line deviates from that of China. We are reminded that Communist ideology does not yet wholly obliterate national sentiments and attitudes, and that the states of the Communist world stand at very different levels of material culture. International communism, in short, is politically polycentric, not monolithic.

THE SOVIET BLOC AND THE DEVELOPING COUNTRIES

The split in the external policies of U.S.S.R. and China is manifested in their approaches to that sizable fraction of mankind which is choosing to adopt a politically neutral attitude towards the great contention of our times. Neutrality has a wide range of meanings: it can signify "rank indifference as well as calculated detachment or rationally controlled impartiality." [5] In a dangerous world, many nations—and not only small ones—seek the means peacefully to develop their economies and to preserve their often newly won

---

[5] Georg Schwarzenburger, "The Scope of Neutralism," *Yearbook of World Affairs, 1961,* Stevens & Sons Ltd. (London), 1961, vol. 15, p. 234.

political independence by resorting to policies of nonalignment or noninvolvement. The number of such nations, which is not small, includes the Indian Union, Burma, Indonesia, Afghanistan, the United Arab Republic, Syria, Iraq, Yugoslavia, Switzerland, Sweden, Austria, and Ireland, as well as many of the newly emerged states of Africa. Moreover, some of these countries, which are widely spread geographically, occupy strategically interesting locations. It is not surprising therefore that both the U.S.S.R. and the western powers have been at pains to woo them. The care and skill which the U.S.S.R. has applied, and is still applying, in its policy towards the uncommitted nations deserves consideration, for it is but one aspect of the challenge which it has thrown down to the West.

Soviet foreign trade. Foreign trade has never occupied the vitally important place in the economy that it does in most parts of the western world, if only because, with its vast and varied resources, the U.S.S.R. is able to move far in pursuit of its traditional policy of economic self-sufficiency. The U.S.S.R.'s foreign trade amounts to only 3 per cent of the gross national product, and two-thirds of it is carried on within the Communist bloc. Although the U.S.S.R.'s volume of trade exceeds the total of all the other Communist countries, the bloc's share of world trade amounts to only about 10 per cent. Foreign trade is conducted there by a government department which is concerned not only with purely commercial considerations but also with the political implications of trade.

Admittedly, the U.S.S.R. has increasingly commanded substantial surpluses of a variety of products which enter into world trade. Among these products we find petroleum and cotton, manganese and chrome ores, gold, platinum, and diamonds, tractors and machine tools, and timber and grain. Despite the great scale and fast pace of its industrialization and partly because of climatic and other limitations imposed on its agriculture, it suffers shortages which can only be counterbalanced by foreign trade. In recent years, such shortages have included merchant and fishing vessels, natural rubber, raw wool, hides and leather, specialized machines (for the textile industry and certain branches of the chemical industry), and tropical foods and beverages. Given its ever-increasing industrial strength, then, the U.S.S.R. can, and clearly intends to, compete vigorously with western suppliers. In its trade dealings in some commodities, the U.S.S.R. cooperates smoothly (and advantageously) with western producers—as it does, for example, in the diamond market. In general it takes account of, and respects, world prices, although it may undercut these on occasion, as it did with petroleum traded to Cuba at prices lower than those of Venezuela, its former supplier. In some products, such as steel, heavy machine tools, petroleum, and tractors, its production costs compare closely or even favorably with those of western suppliers. In others, such as nonferrous metals other than copper, its production costs are so high that their export offers no economic profit. But trade outside the U.S.S.R. is conceived above all as a means of furthering Soviet policy—as a means of supporting its friends, of weakening the developing countries' ties with the West, and of winning adherents to the Soviet system.

Soviet credits. The scale and geographical distribution of credits provide an interesting pointer to Soviet policy towards the outside world. At first, beginning in 1946, they were made to other Communist countries in Europe and Asia: twice as much went to those of Europe as to those of Asia, and since 1957 no further credits have been extended to China. The total of Soviet credits to Communist and economically underdeveloped countries between 1955 and mid-July 1962 was 10,200 million new rubles ($2,550,000,000), of which 76 per cent went to countries of the Communist bloc. The main purpose of these grants is to help the Communist countries reach their production targets. If this effort is successful, the Soviets claim that the bloc will by 1965 account for more than one-half of the world's industrial production. Grants to the so-called uncommitted countries of Asia, Africa, and Latin America have been made since 1954, and on an increasing scale, especially since 1959. The two largest recipients so far are India and the United Arab Republic where the U.S.S.R. has been financing the Aswan High Dam. But the list of recipients is long; it includes Indonesia, Afghanistan,

Pakistan, Nepal, Ceylon, Iraq, Yemen, Ethiopia, the Somali Republic, Guinea, Ghana, Mali, Sudan, Tunisia, Cuba, and Argentina. While the credits cover a wide range of goods, and especially heavy industrial equipment, they finance substantial deliveries of armaments which provide a profitable trade for the U.S.S.R. The United Arab Republic, Indonesia, Cuba, and Iraq have been the chief recipients so far of such military aid.

The Soviet argument is that the newly independent states have not yet thrown off the economic colonialism of the West; that they are passing through a phase of nationalism; and that, if they are given help towards industrialization, this will bring changes in the social structure conducive to a socialist revolution. Soviet help in the form of supplies and technicians is clearly valuable to the underdeveloped countries which lack capital and modern technical skills. Of course, such aid is not altruistic, since the U.S.S.R. hopes for political gains at a later time. The policy is one aspect of the cold war, which is euphemistically called peaceful coexistence, for it is an attempt to beat the capitalist world at its own game. The stakes are high and the issue must remain for some time in doubt. But if the policy succeeds, Moscow's empire, which has failed to embrace Yugoslavia, Albania, and China, will nevertheless extend into all the continents except Australasia.

The Soviet non-ruble offensive. The non-ruble policy of Soviet penetration does not rest solely on the provision of credits with which to buy Russian goods and services. It is supported by such bodies, set up at Moscow, as the Institute for Oriental Studies and the Africa Institute, which began as recently as the end of 1959. These and such similar institutions, in other Communist-bloc states, as China's Institute for Latin American Affairs are investigating the political, economic, and social conditions of the developing countries. Allegedly with a view to reducing international tension and to supporting anticolonialism and anti-imperialism, the U.S.S.R. has tried to rally and lead the Asian and African nations. It has succeeded in creating the Permanent Organization for Afro-Asian Peoples Solidarity, which has its headquarters at Cairo and holds conferences every two years. This organization is only in part Communist; the nature of the solidarity for which it exists may appear in doubt, for there remains little imperialism still to fight. However, it illustrates the initiative, organizing skill, patience, and faith with which the U.S.S.R. works towards its revolutionary aims. Under the aegis of this organization, the U.S.S.R. appears as the champion of peace and promotes peace movements, youth education, women's and writers' organizations, trade unionism (especially in Africa south of the Sahara), and magazine publications. In these various activities the U.S.S.R. is able to make direct contacts (additional to those made through trade and the provision of technical and educational services) with the many developing countries. By such acts as the building of a stadium at Jakarta (Indonesia) for the Asian Olympic Games in 1962 and another at Conakry (Guinea) for the first Pan-African Youth Festival in 1963, the U.S.S.R. seeks to give spectacular demonstration of its support for movements over which it may eventually win control.

It is evident that such activities do not reap easy and immediate harvests. Soviet efforts in Cuba, which is classed as a national democratic state, anti-West and pro-Communist, may be rated highly successful; those in Africa have so far failed. The U.S.S.R. has come to experience what is well known in the West—namely, the ingratitude of those to whom generous credits have been made. This is notably true of the United Arab Republic, where President Nasser has shown an increasingly hostile attitude towards the Communist bloc. Khrushchev initially appeared to alienate the Algerians, also, by withholding his recognition of their Provisional Government. Neither in the Congo nor in Guinea has his policy achieved anything but failure. Indeed, it appears optimistic to believe that the system which has brought political and economic strength, as well as pride and contentment to the peoples of the Soviet Union, should necessarily become the goal of nations elsewhere, for political philosophies and institutions are notoriously, and perhaps inevitably, the products of specific human environments and traditions. "Another's bread is bitter to the taste and his staircase hard to climb." Yet the struggle for the mind of the world, especially that of the uncommitted world, continues. Under centralized governmental control, increasing attention is being paid to the preparatory training (including language study) of engineers, technicians, and party officials to be sent to the developing countries. The newly emerged nations, exploiting the advantages of their policies of non-alignment, should gain from the attentions (and credits) which reach them from both East and West. In short, the nuclear stalemate has produced the cold war of peaceful coexistence, in which the protagonists for world leadership are braced to exert themselves in a struggle where the principal weapons are drawn from the armories of politics, economics, and psychology.

Bibliography

1 Among the many reliable studies of the history of Russia are:

Fisher, R. H. *The Russian Fur Trade, 1500-1700.* Berkeley, Calif.: U. of Calif., 1943.

Pierce, Richard A. *Russian Central Asia, 1867-1917.* Berkeley, Calif.: U. of Calif., 1960.

Skrine, F. H. *The Expansion of Russia, 1815-1900.* (New ed.) Cambridge, England: Cambridge U. P., 1915.

Sumner, B. H. *Peter the Great and the Emergence of Russia.* London: The English Universities Press, 1950.

———. *Survey of Russian History.* London: Duckworth, 1944.

Vernadsky, G. *The Origins of Russia.* Oxford: Clarendon Press, 1959.

2 Some books on the transition from the Russian Empire to the Soviet Union are:

Florinsky, M. T. *The End of the Russian Empire.* New York: Collier, 1961.

Pipes, Richard. *The Formation of the Soviet Union: Communism and Nationalism, 1917-1923.* Cambridge, Mass.: Harvard U. P., 1954.

Seton-Watson, G. H. N. *The Decline of Imperial Russia.* London: Methuen, 1952.

3 Some books on the geography of the U.S.S.R. are:

Balzak, S. S., Vasyutin, V. F., and Feigin, Ya. G. *Economic Geography of the USSR.* New York: Macmillan, 1949. Translated from the Russian, originally published in 1940.

Baransky, N. N. *Economic Geography of the U.S.S.R.* Moscow: Foreign Languages Publishing House, 1956.

Berg, L. S. *Natural Regions of the USSR.* New York: Macmillan, 1950. Translated from the Russian.

Cole, J. P., and German, F. C. *A Geography of the USSR: The Background to a Planned Economy.* London: Butterworths, 1961.

Cressey, George B. *Soviet Potentials: A Geographic Appraisal.* Syracuse, N.Y.: Syracuse U. P., 1962.

East, W. Gordon, and Spate, O. H. K. (eds.). *The Changing Map of Asia: A Political Geography*. 4th ed. New York: Dutton; and London: Methuen, 1961. Chapter 6 deals with the Asiatic USSR.

Hodgkins, J. A. *Soviet Power: Energy Resources, Production and Potentials*. London: Prentice Hall International, 1961.

Hoffman, George W. (ed.). *A Geography of Europe, Including the Asiatic USSR*. 2nd ed. New York: Ronald, 1961. Chapter 9 by Theodore Shabad, "The Soviet Union," pp. 638-728.

Jorré, Georges. *The Soviet Union; The Land and Its People*. 2nd ed. London: Longmans, 1961. Translated from the French and revised by E. D. Laborde.

Mikhailov, Nikolai. *Glimpses of the USSR: Its Economy and Geography*. Moscow: Foreign Language Publishing House, 1960. Translated from the Russian.

Mirov, N. T. *Geography of Russia*. New York: Wiley, 1951.

Saushkin, J. G. *Economic Geography of the Soviet Union*. Oslo, Norway: Oslo U. P., 1956. Eight lectures March-April, 1956 at the Department of Geography, University of Oslo. Translated from the Russian.

Shabad, Theodore. *Geography of the USSR: A Regional Survey*. New York: Columbia U. P., 1951.

4 On specific social aspects of the USSR, the following books are important and informative:

Beaujeu-Garnier, J. *Géographie de la Population*. Paris: Éditions M Th. Genin, 1958. Vol. II, pp. 405-448.

Kennan, George. *Soviet Foreign Policy (1917-1941)*. Princeton, N. J.: Van Nostrand, 1960.

Kolarz, Walter. *Religion in the Soviet Union*. New York: St. Martins; and London: Macmillan, 1961.

———. *Russia and her Colonies*. 2nd ed. London: Philip, 1952.

Konovalov, S. *Russo-Polish Relations*. London: The Cresset Press, 1945.

5 On the nature and progress of the USSR's economy:

Economic Survey of Europe, 1961. Part I. Chapt. II, "The European Economy in 1961," Geneva: United Nations, 1962.

Forty Years of Soviet Power in Facts and Figures. Moscow: Foreign Languages Publishing House, 1958.

Soviet Handbook 1959-1965. Soviet Booklet, No. 57. London: 1959. This gives an outline, with statistics, of the current plan.

Jasny, Naum, *The Socialized Agriculture of the USSR*. Stanford, Calif.: Stanford U. P., 1949.

Maynard, Sir John. *The Russian Peasant and Other Studies*. London: Victor Gollancz, 1942.

Schwartz, Harry. *Russia's Soviet Economy*. London: Jonathan Cape, 1951.

Taaffe, Robert, *Rail Transportation and the Economic Development of Soviet Central Asia*. Department of Geography Research Paper No. 64. Chicago: U. of Chicago, 1960.

6 Some books on the geopolitical aspect of the U.S.S.R. are:

East, W. Gordon, and Moodie, A. E. (eds.). *The Changing World: Studies in Political Geography*. Yonkers-on-Hudson, N. Y.: World Book; and London: Harrap, 1956.

Jackson, W. A. Douglas. *The Russo-Chinese Borderlands*. Searchlight Book No. 2. Princeton, N. J.: Van Nostrand, 1962.

Lattimore, Owen. *Inner Asian Frontiers of China*. New York: American Geographical Society, 1940, 1951.

Mackinder, Sir Halford J. *Democratic Ideals and Reality: A Study in the Politics of Reconstruction*. London: Constable; and New York: Holt, 1919. Reprinted, 1942. London: Pelican Books, 1944.

7 On the Northern Sea route, there are in English two comparable and competent studies:

Armstrong, Terence. *The Northern Sea Route: Soviet Exploitation of the North East Passage*. Cambridge, England: Cambridge U. P., 1952.

Krypton, Constantine. *The Northern Sea Route and the Economy of the Soviet North*. Research Program on the USSR, Studies No. 14. London: Methuen, 1956.

8 Regional treatisies include:

Armstrong, Terence. *The Russians in the Arctic: Aspects of Soviet Exploration and Exploitation of the Far North, 1937-1957*. London: Methuen, 1958.

Lied, Jonas. *Siberian Arctic*. London: Methuen, 1960.

Suslov, S. P. *Physical Geography of Asiatic Russia*. San Francisco: W. H. Freeman, 1961. Translated from the Russian.

Index